"In the midst of incessant noise and relentless texts, tweets and emails, *A Spirituality of Listening* offers an accessible and welcome respite. With an obvious respect for Scripture and tradition, Anderson provides a contemporary, relevant and fresh perspective on the difficult practice of listening. Transcending evangelical, mainline and Roman Catholic categories with honesty, vulnerability and realness, Keith writes as one who has listened with discipline and has heard the voice of God."

Tisa Lewis, retired senior director, The Association of Theological Schools in the United States and Canada

"*A Spirituality of Listening* invites the reader to take the leap into the wondrous ways to listen. In so doing, it offers a salve for the soul that leads us to experience God in a way that permeates and illuminates every aspect of life. Refreshing, relevant and timely."

Romanita Hairston, vice president, US programs, World Vision

"Many people are on a journey to find new practices of Christian spirituality—meaningful ways to know God and to reflect God's love faithfully in their lives. Keith Anderson provides reflections and practical guidance for this journey out of his lifetime of listening to God, reading spiritual guides from across the centuries and practicing what he has heard and discovered. *A Spirituality of Listening* is a wise and encouraging invitation to listen in order to hear God speaking in every part of our lives."

Jo-Ann Badley, dean of theology, Ambrose University

A
SPIRITUALITY
OF LISTENING
LIVING WHAT WE HEAR

KEITH R. ANDERSON

FOREWORD BY DAN B. ALLENDER

IVP Books

An imprint of InterVarsity Press
Downers Grove, Illinois

InterVarsity Press
P.O. Box 1400, Downers Grove, IL 60515-1426
ivpress.com
email@ivpress.com

InterVarsity Press® is the book-publishing division of InterVarsity Christian Fellowship/USA®, a movement of students and faculty active on campus at hundreds of universities, colleges and schools of nursing in the United States of America, and a member movement of the International Fellowship of Evangelical Students. For information about local and regional activities, visit intervarsity.org.

Scripture quotations, unless otherwise noted, are from the New Revised Standard Version of the Bible, copyright 1989 by the Division of Christian Education of the National Council of the Churches of Christ in the USA. Used by permission. All rights reserved.

While any stories in this book are true, some names and identifying information may have been changed to protect the privacy of individuals.

Cover design: Cindy Kiple
Interior design: Beth McGill
Images: © snvv/iStockphoto

ISBN 978-0-8308-4609-2 (print)
ISBN 978-0-8308-9920-3 (digital)

Printed in the United States of America ∞

Library of Congress Cataloging-in-Publication Data
Names: Anderson, Keith, 1949-
Title: A spirituality of listening : living what we hear / Keith R. Anderson
 ; foreword by Dan B. Allender.
Description: Downers Grove : InterVarsity Press, 2016. | Includes
 bibliographical references and index.
Identifiers: LCCN 2015040189 (print) | LCCN 2015041773 (ebook) | ISBN
 9780830846092 (pbk. : alk. paper) | ISBN 9780830899203 (eBook)
Subjects: LCSH: Listening--Religious aspects--Christianity.
Classification: LCC BV4647.L56 A53 2016 (print) | LCC BV4647.L56 (ebook) |
 DDC 231.7--dc23
LC record available at http://lccn.loc.gov/2015040189

P	21	20	19	18	17	16	15	14	13	12	11	10	9	8	7	6	5	4	3	2	1
Y	33	32	31	30	29	28	27	26	25	24	23	22	21	20	19	18	17	16			

To Wendy:

Because you alone know the meaning of the words:
"Now instead of two stories fumbling to meet,
we belong to one story that the two, joining, made."

Wendell Berry

◇◆◇

CONTENTS

FOREWORD

Dan B. Allender

◇◆◇

I T WAS EARLY SEPTEMBER 2009 and it was the first time
I sat in the office of the new president of The Seattle School
of Theology & Psychology. Keith Anderson had been president
for less than three months. I asked him, "What is the first order
of business for you in your first one hundred days?" He didn't
smile. He answered: "You."

I thought he was joking. Keith's skin is mostly hidden behind
a salty, no nonsense, almost curmudgeonly beard, but I could see
the reddishness of his intensity. He was not joking. A quixotic
playfulness passed over his face, but his gaze was resolute. "You
are my major focus for the first one hundred and perhaps several
hundred days." I simply asked, "Why?"

"I don't know how you will play. You have gone from being
the president to being faculty. I don't know how you will handle
being led—you have never been my employee." Then he added,
"If you are going to remain in this school and know joy, then you
need to let me help you shepherd your legacy."

I was looking forward to catching up with a friend and within minutes I was asked to consider the viability and trajectory of my future at The Seattle School. It was a brief conversation that would change the direction of my life. And it all came about because Keith Anderson has a deep, passionate, holy heart to explore terrain that most fear to tread.

If you were to hear Keith speak about himself you would hear the self-deprecation of a good Baptist grandson of Swedish immigrants. There are few that can out-work him and he is loyal to a fault. In many ways, I sense he comes from another world— one where your word is troth and your truth is an oath to love. His pursuit of knowledge and wisdom is equally a desire to be faithful to the many living and dead who have shaped his heart and mind. He is a man that I would follow to storm the gates of hell if he asked.

And he asked if I could play well and be led by him. It was premature to say I can and will, but I knew in my heart that few get the privilege in this life to work for a person whose words are fundamentally true to his heart. I have said to Keith more times than I can count: "You must write more."

When I see an email from Keith to the board or student body, I hungrily read each word because Keith cherishes words and the form in which they come. What is said is both beautiful and compelling. I recall the day when Keith told me that a new labor of love was finished. I implored for the opportunity to read.

This book is about listening. Few listen well. It is not a hip category or skill that permeates the cultural or academic conversation. It is given at best a polite head nod, the way we might meet an aged man or woman as we offer them our seat on public transportation. We give listening a seat but we don't deign to ask it a single question.

Listening requires a heart that is humble enough to move slowly through the cadence of another's speech. It requires the courage to risk asking and then the even greater risk of waiting for patterns to occur that illumine what is being said. Listening is the holy work of attuning one's soul to the accumulation of meaning that comes only to those who tend to speech like a midwife. It is art and skill, knowledge and wisdom.

Listening requires fierce quietness. Keith Anderson is a fiercely humble, kind and generous man who will help you receive the blessing of attunement. Keith writes in a manner that is accessible but also invites you to join him on a theologically rich trek up his beloved Mount Rainer. The journey is demanding and at times stunning and dangerous. The benefit is the certainty that your heart will become larger and your capacity for meaningful connection with God and others enriched.

I have worked for Keith now for six years. I hope to do so for many more. His ability to listen to my heart has enabled me to discover the greater calling of the kingdom of God for my last few decades on this earth. I am his debtor for a lifetime of listening and now I am thankful that you get to listen to the beauty of his words and life. You too will never be the same.

one

RESONANCE

Another Way of Listening

*Telling a story is like reaching into a granary full of
wheat and drawing out only a handful. There is
always more to tell than can be told.*

WENDELL BERRY

◇◆◇

I HAVE SPENT MY LIFE in the Gospels listening to Jesus. I
have watched him and tried to listen and learn. I have
tripped over his words as often as I have found the way, but I
am drawn again and again to listen. Sometimes I wonder if I
make things more difficult than they need to be. What I can't
shake is the feeling that I have lived my life in a kind of presence
because of the words. Like Wendell Berry's words above, I am
drawn to listening because I have a hunch that "there is always
more to tell than can be told."[1]

And so I decided to write about listening. I have looked for
simplicity in the midst of the complexity of the words. My

mistake has been to forget that the Scriptures are a narrative of people who lived in time and space. It is their story of how they listened to the one they called God. My mistake has been to silence the thunder that wanted to be heard while I did all the talking about what I thought the voice had said. I don't think I'm alone in this. Raised to believe certain things about God, Scripture and faith. Convinced of the rightness of that way of thinking. Able even to raise my hands in worship to show I can feel the music. But not so sure what happened along the way. Did I lose my way? Did something change? There are times I wonder how much of my spirituality was living a culture of faith in a certain way. I wonder if I became an expert at the forms of faith but not the heart. Prayer, worship, Scripture, meditation and Bible studies—all of these I know well. Why, then, do I sometimes feel something was lost, muted or silenced along the way? I know I am not alone.

Learning to Listen

I have spent my life in the church or nearby. I have held the microphone of religion and faith in my hands, preaching, teaching, writing and using many words. I wonder now if I practiced listening as well as I practiced my own use of words. I wonder if I took for granted that listening should come first. So I set out to wander in the texts, practices and forms that shaped the life of Jesus and the community that formed him. There are centuries-deep practices that are more common and familiar than I once thought. Not surprisingly, there is an insistent theme of listening. More than a call to certain practices or disciplines, there is an invitation to an orientation of one's life to a universe that is alive with presence and voice, always with "more that can be told."

Most of us take the science of sound and hearing for granted. Something emits energy in the form of a vibration. Pressure creates a wave, which finds its way to the ear where it is filtered to the ear drum and sent to the brain. The volume and pitch of sound waves vary based on many factors—the source of the sound, the amount and type of energy that generated it, and the environment in which the waves are received. Words like *amplitude, frequency, pitch, acoustics, ossicles, cochlea* and *audiology* are all the lexicon of hearing. Science tells us we walk through a universe alive with sound waves and electrical impulses, all of which have something to do with compressed air. Some theorize that sound is heard in the very cells of our body. We know that infants respond to sound in the womb. We also know that sound resonates with our bodies in certain ways that actually lower the heart rate, decrease respiration and contribute to healing. If we could see the waves, we would see zig-zagging intersections of waves in every possible direction. We would see that the universe is alive in ways we do not recognize without an imagination for listening.

I am no expert in listening. I am no expert in spirituality. I am, however, a lover of words, stories and listening: words because they are the wings of relationship; stories because the very heart of Christian faith is the story of Jesus' life, death and resurrection; and listening because it is one way I know God (not the only way, but one way). Every once in a while it happens: I have the feeling I am part of a conversation that was and is and is still to come. I have the feeling that the universe is more alive than I usually notice. I have the feeling there is a voice to be heard if I can relearn to listen.

So, I write because I want to learn how to listen all over again. I write because I believe there is another way of listening. I have a feeling that something I lost along the way was the simple, everyday experience of conversation with God. I write because I think you might want to do that too. My hope is to stir in us all a longing to listen for the voice of God in everything. I know a statement like that might send some readers packing because they can't believe in a claim that simple. I am a student of spirituality and a teacher as well. I have read hundreds of books and pondered dozens of images of spirituality, but this one, this capacity or practice of listening is deeply grounded in all writings on all forms of spirituality. However, its simplicity doesn't mean it's automatic or easy.

What lives in this book from front to back are questions I cannot escape. I've tried to get away from them, but I find they won't let me go. There is one particularly persistent question: Does God continue to have something to say in the twenty-first century?

On a recent trip I pulled into the parking lot behind Bread and Chocolate, my favorite coffee shop in St. Paul, Minnesota. The large parking lot is shared with a church that displayed a large sign declaring their answer: God is still speaking. It was remarkable because it read as though it was an announcement or a secret that was being revealed. But I understand. Many of us believe God spoke in the first century and perhaps even in the twentieth century, when the church was the platform for God's voice to be heard. But what about now? The answer is no longer clear in a century when the church is losing its voice in much of the Western world and in a culture when generations of people have lost confidence in the church. We live in a nation where old certitudes are fading or gone and a time when spirituality is often just a way to sell exercise equipment, music and even relationships. It is a time of great skepticism about spirituality that insists the question be raised: Is it possible to claim that we are people who can learn to listen to God? The accepted view of popular culture is that it's one thing to pray, to talk *to* God, but to make the claim that you hear God speak implies you are crazy.

Biblical spirituality says there is still a source that reveals the voice of the living God. It asserts that God is not done with the business of revelation and creation but instead continues to have something to say and something yet to be accomplished in the very culture that isn't sure if God is done speaking. We have muted, muffled and, in some cases, silenced the voice of God because we have forgotten to listen in the ways and places where God's voice has always been heard. I hope to recover a way of practicing spirituality that has been silenced for some because we have lost our listening; we need to re-create another way of listening. And I confess, I am not only a product of a culture that silenced the thunder of God's voice; I have myself done it for others. I don't sit in any seat outside looking in from a comfortable perch; I have helped to foster practices and a culture of silence.

In an earlier time of my life, there was a question that blared its answer on radio, TV, magazines, pulpits and talk shows across North America. Started as a question in academia, it soon was asked on street corners and in libraries, coffee shops and offices: "Is God dead?" Philosophers, theologians and curious onlookers concluded yes. I listened in on the conversations too, and I wonder: Did God pass away in the night, or over the centuries as humankind outgrew our need for an all-powerful deity? Did God die because we found new technologies, medications and innovations to replace God as creator, healer and redeemer? It never seemed to me to be a question about God as much as about people. Some answer that we simply outgrew the need for

God. Others answer that we now find enough in our own voices to replace the word of God. And some answer that God exists, but only in us—God is ultimately *only* found in individual human-human interactions—between an *I* and a *Thou*. And for many, we simply ran out of energy for the machinery that had always supported God—the infrastructure of modernism, the hegemony of the church, and the voice of an educated, ordained and authoritative clergy.

I wonder.

Even in Seattle, a city nourished by what I call REI spirituality, a coalition of environmentalism, social consciousness and tolerance for all differences, I still find a hunger for something that isn't filled by our care of Mother Earth or the poor or certain other marginalized peoples. Perhaps the question in our day is no longer "Is God dead?" but "*Where* can God's voice be heard?" Most people aren't really fooled by the notion that humanity is all that exists, that humanity is the final answer to the questions asked across the centuries. I find that most people are hungry for something more, something deeper, something beyond. In my experience most people believe that God is alive, but they wonder if God has lost his voice. Sermons speak of almost everything except a continuing conversation with a living God. Books, articles, blogs and social media are full of the continuing search for the Spirit that has been our human quest from the beginning; we readily speak *about* God or *for* God when it seems our longing is to speak *with* God.

Where can God's voice be heard today? Some say God's voice can only be heard in the Bible, where the history of what God said is recorded, as if God cut off all communication after the early second century. Others believe God can only be heard in human-to-human relationships, as if the transcendent God of the ages can no longer speak for God's own self. For some there is a notion that God can only be heard through educated and certified voices trained in special ways that authorize their words, as if God's voice must be filtered through certain people. And some say that God can only be heard through rituals, liturgies or gatherings where particular forms contain the voice of God, as if God's exclusive concern is with religion, worship, sermons, praise choruses and hymns.

You can tell that I'm not buying any of this because there was one who showed us another way to listen. His name was Yeshua, or Jesus as he is known to most of us. Early followers made outrageous claims that he not only spoke *for* God but he knew God and even *was* God wrapped up in a human body, which certainly complicates things. The entire weight of the Bible tilts the story to him. It says that Jesus knew something we need:

He was in the world,
the world was there through him,
and yet the world didn't even notice.
He came to his own people,
but they didn't want him.
But whoever did want him,
who believed he was who he claimed
and would do what he said,
He made to be their true selves,
their child-of-God selves. (John 1:10-12 *The Message*)

Jesus is the pattern or archetype of spirituality as it shapes people into our "child-of-God selves." A teacher named Paul said, "He is the image of the invisible God, the firstborn of all creation. . . . For in him all the fullness of God was pleased to dwell" (Colossians 1:15, 19). Listening for the voice of God is not simply waiting for an audible voice; it is also spending time in the presence of the teacher, Jesus, whose teaching speaks loud enough for all of us to hear. Eugene Peterson said it as economically as anyone: "Jesus is the way God comes to us. Jesus is the way we come to God."[2]

THE RESONANT SOUND OF GOD'S VOICE

In conversation with a colleague we talked about God's presence as a resonant sound. It was a new concept to me. In some musical forms there is a baseline of melodic sound that resounds through the entire song. The orchestra interacts with the baseline in a dynamic interplay—a resonance to the initiating primary tones called *cantus primus*. It is not a simple echo that returns the sound it was given, but a complex point and counterpoint. It is a melodic interaction that starts the a baseline of music, upon which other tones interact in interdependence on the starting line. *Cantus primus*, most simply put, says there is "a fixed line of melody to which other voices are added."[3] Like the ancient plain chant or Gregorian chants in the fourteenth century, there is a "fixed song" to which the rest of the musicians respond. The baseline of music is always present, active and living, and in a technical way I do not understand, the originating musician leaves space for new melodies to be created.

That idea is similar to what I mean by the voice of God present in all things. God comes to us in Jesus through the Spirit. God has spoken; God speaks still. Human spirituality is ongoing responsiveness and interaction with what is revealed. That's good theology. God "intrudes" into human history and our stories as unrelenting love. There is nothing passive about any of this—we don't make it happen—we say yes. And, like the *cantus firmus*, we respond to what has been given voice by Father,

Son and Holy Spirit as we participate in co-creative listening. Does it come as the sound like a human voice? I can't say it always does; I can't even say that it often does, but there is a way of living in faith that issues a defiant conviction that God's word is heard in surprisingly common and ordinary ways. I have come to think of it as a kind of resonance. What starts in one place as a sound or experience becomes an ongoing vibration and movement of sound. Resonance is also a strong emotional association with a place, story, person or memory. Something starts the movement and it resonates in another. It is dynamic, alive, co-creative and responsive: we must be aware, show up, pay attention, participate and engage that which is heard. Resonance is another way of listening to creation, everyday life, story and memory, prophetic thunder, lament and Jesus himself. In the exercise of faith, we hear and see differently.

Another metaphor to describe this might be the ballast of a ship. Ballast is not an anchor that keeps you in port or secured to a single location in a harbor. Rather, it is substance below the surface, weighty enough to keep the ship afloat. Ballast is that which can balance the ship so that navigation is possible, but ballast doesn't tell you where you must go like the voice in my GPS, which directs every turn on my way to a pre-determined location. Ballast keeps the ship afloat as we navigate, poorly or well, on journeys both planned and spontaneous. Without ballast, a ship will spin wildly in place or twist and turn in every wind and eventually sink because that which is on the surface overwhelms the physics of the ship in motion. Listening is ballast for all spirituality. Simply put, God's words are the ballast, the reference point. But it comes to us as something intensely and intimately relational, what I prefer to call conversational. It isn't something we control and make happen; it is something we receive as we wait in trust and readiness to what God will reveal to open ears and hearts.

I think I got waylaid early on in my theological education by the word *revelation*; I thought it meant I would be given answers, information and truth. Once I had those things I could set up shop as an independent contractor who gave others answers, information and truth. Instead, revelation has come to mean a resonant conversation with God as I have lived my life in an ongoing relationship with Jesus. Along the way I have encountered answers, information and even truth, but more often I have been invited to continue to listen in ways that are common and more familiar than I expected. My claim is simple: spirituality is grounded in ordinary life experiences. We need to learn to listen to rhythms of life, narratives and creation. I also make a more complex claim: Jesus learned to know God through biblical forms still available to us. John Calvin said God "clothes himself, so to speak, with the image of the world, in which he would present himself to our contemplation. . . . Therefore, as soon as the name of God sounds in our ears, or the thought of him occurs to our minds, let the world become our school if we desire rightly to know God."[4]

These forms of spirituality are not ethereal, otherworldly and abstract; they are earthy, grounded and clothed in our lives embodied in time and space. So I set out to consider Jesus' own incarnated journey toward faith. I wanted to see what I could find about his culture, the story of his people and the unfolding of practices that are centuries deep. I looked to the *forms* of spirituality, or what might better be called the practices that formed faith in ancient Israel and in Jesus. There are rhythms to life and practices of listening that earlier generations called obedience, discipleship, worship and spirituality. Today there is a new spirituality that struggles with these kind of words but still longs for an experience of presence and voice.

I am captivated more by something humanity has practiced deeply over time than I am by the latest innovation in spirituality. Learning to listen is one way to understand Jesus' own formation and teaching. How did Jesus come to learn God? He did, you know. He wasn't born fully formed but grew in faith, even as he was formed intellectually, emotionally and physically. How did Jesus come to know God? There are many answers, but one seems loudest to me: Jesus learned to listen for God, to pay attention in his life as he lived it in his neighborhood. For some, the work of listening to God's voice feels like unknowable terrain requiring a map, and some reach for the simplest map they can find. I prefer instead to see this work in the spirit of attentive, contemplative curiosity.

The wisdom poetry of the book of Proverbs asks and answers its own questions:

> Does not wisdom call,
>   and does not understanding raise her voice?
> On the heights, beside the way,
>   at the crossroads she takes her stand;
> beside the gates in front of the town,
>   at the entrance of the portals she cries out:
> "To you, O people, I call,
>   and my cry is to all that live.
> O simple ones, learn prudence;
>   acquire intelligence, you who lack it.
> Hear, for I will speak noble things,
>   and from my lips will come what is right."
>   (Proverbs 8:1-6)

I long for us to "eavesdrop" on those whose passion for God compelled them to listen to God speaking in the most ordinary and sometimes extraordinary moments. The poet wrote, "The hearing ear and the seeing eye—the Lord has made them both" (Proverbs 20:12). I've rediscovered in Scripture another way of listening that erupts into boisterous wonder. Listening in wonder sounds romantic I suppose, but it isn't always a kind of ethereal delight. It often starts with another form of wonder: confusion. "I wonder what's going on?" is an honest way of listening in wonder. It might start with uncertainty that leads to curiosity. It may be playful or vexing, but there is an instinct to make sense out of what we hear. That's the invitation of the pages that lie ahead. I'm not taken much by formulas for listening—"ten steps on how to hear the voice of God" or "seven principles for successful spiritual practices in the twenty-first century." What I have found instead is that life is found in the details. And life is sometimes lost because of the details. My conviction is that wisdom still cries out if we can learn how and where to listen—on the heights, along the way, beside the gates and at the entrance of the portals. Some of my own story inhabits these pages, but this is not a spiritual memoir or running commentary on the details of my own spiritual practices or experiences. It is instead, I would like to think, a way to enter a conversation that began long before my story was told and will continue long after I am gone.

Jayber Crow, the title character of Wendell Berry's novel of the same name, returned to the childhood community of Port William. He found a perch where he could listen and remember. "What would come, came."[5] Memories of family and those who had raised him after the death of his parents. Barns, stores, henhouses, steamboats and the river. He more felt than heard their memory, but he knew himself in the presence of those who had loved him. "I remembered so plainly that I could *hear* the sound of hammer shaping metal on an anvil."[6] He knew himself to be in the presence. No audible voices. No mystical visions. No unexpected epiphanies (appearances). But presence. And then this: "I saw that, for me, this country would always be populated with presences and absences, presences of absences, the living and the dead. The world as it is would always be a reminder of the world as it was, and of the world that is to come."[7] My hope is that the pages you hold in your hand will offer a similar perch to listen and remember.

PRACTICE LISTENING: THE REFLECTIVE PAUSE

One form listening might take is the *practice of the reflective pause.* In the midst of the day, prompt yourself to take sixty seconds to breathe slowly and reflect. It's not a complicated technology but a daily practice. Ask your own set of questions that will help you reflect on what is going on around you. "What am I feeling about the day so far?" "I wonder if God has something for me to hear or see today." "Where do I sense there is something for me to see, hear or do that seems to come from God?" My own practice is to start the day at my desk with a moment for reflective pause. Before I jump into morning emails, my to-do list and every other list, I take a moment to listen. You might call it prayer, but I ask God to help me listen for his voice in the work that is on my desk and that will come. I ask God to help me pay attention to people, scheduled events and interruptions.

The practice of the reflective pause is possible in the daily rhythms of our lives—just a moment for reflection. What have I *heard* in the last hours of my busy day? That's it. Listening is response to the already active presence of God. If that's true at all, then God has been active in the day already. The posture of listening is not about a physical posture as much as a posture of intent. People have always found that listening prayer is helped by sitting up straight in a chair with hands open on one's lap facing upward in a posture of receptivity while breathing deeply and slowly and waiting. But Mary's response to the angel (messenger) reflects a posture of intent. "Let it be to me as you have said." If there is a perfect prayer, that has to be it. "Let it be." I go along, I am ready to listen, receive and accept. I say yes, God, yes.

two

FIRST WORDS

Listening to Creation

Our goal should be to live life in radical amazement, . . .
get up in the morning and look at the world in a way that
takes nothing for granted. Everything is phenomenal;
everything is incredible; never treat life casually.
To be spiritual is to be amazed.

ABRAHAM HESCHEL

◇◆◇

EVERY DAY AT NINE, NOON AND THREE, I am forced to do something against my will. I work in a 110-year-old building on the Seattle waterfront, converted from a fish-processing plant to a luggage manufacturing plant and now to a theological graduate school where three hundred students walk the same floors that fishermen once traversed. Three times each day there are chimes that ring, and I am forced to listen to the sound.

When we moved into the building we started this practice of chimes as a kind of monastic impulse. We call it "Nine, noon and three: rhythms of prayer." The chimes disrupt meetings and classes. They intrude into board meetings and important conversations. They interrupt our work because you cannot ignore them. We sound the chimes because we know it is hard to stop and even harder to listen. We ring the bells to embody our belief that God is free to intrude into our work at any given moment. We make the sound because we believe our work is done in the presence of the living God, even when we aren't sure we want to listen.

Hearing is a universal human *experience*. Even the deaf can feel vibrations or sense presence. Listening is a universal human *capacity*, but listening isn't easy. Listening isn't always something we want to do. I've become fascinated by our capacity for hearing in recent years. Now in my sixties, I am losing capacity to hear in one ear. It comes in handy when I'm being told something I really don't want to hear. It's convenient when I need a good excuse to miss a deadline or just prefer not to have definite instructions for something I might not want to do. It doesn't mean I can't hear at all in the "bad ear," I just sometimes can't tell you what the words are. I might hear sounds, muffled words and intonations. To hear the words, I must turn my face and my good ear to the speaking voice. That makes it, for me, a metaphor for spirituality—we turn our face so we can hear again. We turn our face in a new direction so the words have meaning and are not merely sounds.

Something happens when we listen; something is released. I know of no other way to describe it. Something is animated, it is physical—brain functions take over as acoustical sounds enter the airwaves—but it is more, much more. Some speak of holy listening. I have experienced listening as holy, but I wonder if the words turn people away. There is distrust for the holy, or at least for the facile way it is talked about. There is disdain for the constant message of fear, shame and contempt for our humanity. There is distrust for a spiritualty that requires sacred spaces, a new lexicon of sacred words, and qualified, certified and trained guides who alone are the master teachers of spirituality. Jesus is the one who fits that role for me, but I wonder how his voice has become muted by the spirituality of a special elite. I wonder how it can be restored. Listening cannot be made into a commodity and sold; it is available to people of all places, ages, genders, race ethnicity and economic classes. Listening is a universal capacity. Holy listening is a practice that is available to all.

Rather than deadly predictability or banal religiosity, the universe is blazing with an excess of wonder to be heard, seen, touched, tasted and desired. I want to hear what is being said by God in my neighborhood and in the ordinary routines of the day. I want to know God all over again, and I think that desire grows out of listening. It has taken on an aura of otherworldly mystery that only a monastic might understand. We believe God is mostly interested in religion, so we relegate it to certain times and places. Instead there is the wild alternative that God is present in the ordinary. My local ice cream shop advertises its delicacy on their logo with the words "Life deserves extraordinary." It motivates me to eat their ice cream, but I think they're off the mark on their philosophy. I say instead, "Ordinary life can be extraordinary." First we listen, and in our listening the ordinary takes on the sense of the extraordinary, of something more.

A sacrament is a ritual or ordinary thing like bread, water or wine that becomes a way to experience the presence of God. It it something common that points to the sacred. Eucharist, or Communion, and baptism can be remarkable moments in which God's presence is celebrated and God's voice is heard. What makes them sacramental is the mystery of the ordinary being transformed into the extraordinary. Spiritual teachers have always understand this: life is sacramental when we learn to discern God and to the voice of God in common, physical things. Life becomes sacramental when we receive ordinary moments with openness to the possibility of mystery. I wonder why we have become resistant to or intolerant of mystery.

A seminary professor spoke recently about Scripture from the perspective of an African culture. She said, "My people in Ghana are comfortable with the biblical world because it is a world of enchantment and mystery, and they experience life that way." God speaks, people are healed, miracles take place, and demons are exorcised. In the West we emphasize Jesus' words and his teachings, but in the global South, there is a lively encounter with what Jesus did, the actions of his life. An enchanted world isn't the same as a Disney or Steven Spielberg production; it is a way of hearing, seeing and discovering the world of Spirit. In the West we often settle for something almost inert when we set aside a biblical worldview in favor of a view of the world that is flat, one-dimensional, predictable, and common. "Life deserves extraordinary" invites us to listen in the most ordinary moments with the faith that God has something more to say here and now.

Listening to God's first words in Genesis sets the stage for the oral culture that develops through the Old Testament all the way to the life of Jesus and the apostle John.

LISTEN FOR THE WORDS THAT ARE SPOKEN

Immersed in such a universe, the ancient Jewish culture learned Torah (Scripture) by listening to its words read orally, recited and repeated. It was a culture where *reading* mostly meant *listening*. They didn't carry portable versions of Torah with them. Young Jewish boys memorized and recited aloud the words of God (Torah) and the Word of God (revelation or God's self-disclosure); they literally did what the psalmist-poet meant when he said, "Thy word have I hid in mine heart" (Psalm 119:11 KJV). By hearing the words read aloud, they memorized them and thus came to know their meaning. Jesus himself learned to know God first by listening. One of the frequent Old Testament phrases about listening starts with the words "Thus says the Lord." So listen for the words that are spoken.

This kind of listening calls for a response from people ready to listen like Samuel, who said, "Speak, for your servant is listening" (1 Samuel 3:10). The root form of the word *listen* in Greek gives us our word "acoustic," with its sense of sound, hearing, apprehension of sound, awareness. And all forms of the word start with the experience of listening to something or someone.

To read Scripture in that culture started by listening to it being read. It was a sensate experience. Sound was transferred from voice to ear. In an oral culture, listening is practiced and learned. So it turns out they knew some of the first words of Torah. You might be surprised by what they heard. The feast of creation with its riotous color, alluring beauty and boundless energy begins with the simplicity of *speech*, "Then God said . . ." The starting place is in those words: *God said.* They are words of irrepressible importance for how we learn to live with God in a world of voices, sounds, presence, music and silence. Imagine a world alive with mystery. Imagine a world where something more is going on than what we see and hear. Listening means that someone is speaking. In listening, there is both giving and receiving, hearing and telling.

Raised in that oral culture, Jesus too was captivated by listening, and it shaped him as teacher. He taught his students through stories crafted in the moment from his surroundings. Jesus radicalized life from an experience of banality to one filled with kingdom expectations, and offered up the ordinary as a classroom of wonder. His most important teachings were about farmers sowing seeds, women sweeping their doorway, and children, sheep, vines, water, bread and barns. To make his point he punctuated his stories with a sudden turn of phrase, "He who has ears to hear, let him hear; she who has eyes to see, let her see." I wonder about that repetition of words. Why did he repeat that phrase to his disciples as many as eight times in the Gospels? Could it be they were especially bad listeners, particularly dense students or just like rowdy children in the third-grade classroom? Could it be they lacked spiritual depth or commitment enough to learn the words the first time? While I think all of the above might be possible, it turns out Jesus himself had simply learned to listen, to have ears to hear.

A CLASSROOM OF WONDER

God *spoke* creation into being: light, a dome in the midst of the waters, dry land, vegetation, the sky, living creatures and humankind. It sets into motion a staggering conviction that the universe is, from the beginning, a place of presence and voice. Eugene Peterson said, "The characteristic element of Square One is this: God said. . . . For Christians, basic spirituality is not only a noun, *God,* but also a verb, *Said* (or *Says*)."[1]

God said. There is an insistence in the simplicity of that phrase. Life starts with someone else taking the first step. The timeline does not start with us. There is a movement toward us; our work is harder—to learn to listen for the voice of God as God walks the landscape of what God created. We don't speak first; first, we listen.

So we go to the narratives of the beginning and, if we are honest, what we find is unexpected. Genesis is not a conversation *about* creation with the Creator. It is part one of conversation *with* the Creator-Author. That is the surprise of creation. It is also the beginning of spirituality. The creation text is not a lesson in something; it is a moment of encounter. It is the beginning of conversation. It is the surprising presence of someone who has something to say. The voice of God in creation is the first evidence of God's love, respect and honor of those who will listen. Listening is our own response of love, respect and honor, not only of each other but of God. It sets into motion for us the capacity to listen, to be empty, curious, waiting and attentive. In listening all of those qualities are necessary:

- We empty our agenda and voice to give ear to another.
- We are curious, expectant, engaged and ready for the other to speak.
- We wait, not intrusive and interruptive but in anticipation.
- We attend to the other, alert, aware, ready to encounter change.
- We are present to the presence of the other; we "show up."
- In it's most simple form: we pay attention.

This is what it means to listen intentionally. "The ears are always on." I don't know who said that, but it's true; there is no on/off

switch for our ears as there is for our headphones. Hearing is not
an option. Sound is always present, noise is everywhere, and we
hear sounds 24-7, yes, even as we sleep. But listening is an active
skill that requires intentionality. We don't have an on/off switch
for our ears, but we need to activate our *listening*. There is a
"letting go" in this kind of listening. I have come to think of listening as an exploration of spirit—an emptying of distractions
and noise that gives my soul space to hear what is there. It may
take a lifetime of practice. I know I cannot force my ears to listen,
but I can make space for listening to astonish me with presence.

The universe is a classroom for curiosity, wonder, learning and
conversation. Because God is the one who speaks, listening
creates the possibility of revelation in all places and at any time.
One of my friends, Tony, says, "I want to live a life of constant
amazement." "Standing on tiptoes" is another way to put it.
Mike Yaconelli wrote a book called *Dangerous Wonder: The Ad-
venture of Childlike Faith*. His chapter headings are provocative:
"Dangerous Wonder," "Risky Curiosity," "Wild Abandon,"
"Daring Playfulness," "Wide-Eyed Listening," "Irresponsible
Passion," "Happy Terror," "Naïve Grace" and "Childlike Faith."
That's the kind of daily spirituality that was spoken into being
in the act of creation.

Since the world is a classroom for learning, as we learn to
listen a process is set into motion that will last all of our lives.
The world is a place thick with presence; it is not tame, predictable, banal and domestic. Some have called this reality
mystery. The ancients called it *mysterium tremendum*, overwhelming mystery, a numinous place. If that's the universe in
which we live, then faith is more about asking curious questions than finding settled answers. Not every question is given
an answer. There is power, the ancients taught us, in *not*

knowing, or at least in knowing we don't know it all. And all spiritual teachers tutor us in the wonder of listening. In spirituality we are all always beginners, living in readiness to take the next step. Jesus said, "Let the children come to me." It is not only in the sophistication of our minds but in the simplicity of our souls that we listen.

THE UNREPEATABLE DRAMA

When the voice of the Creator spoke, change occurred in an unrepeatable drama. In the creation stories we are taken to time before there was time, to place before there was place. We are taken, in fact, to the imagination, intention and integrity in the mind of the Creator-Author. When a novelist sets out to narrate a story, there is a moment for imagination and intention. For some writers, it is a kind of trembling moment of waiting for the first words to be written, the words that will launch the story. For others it is a moment of joy waiting to be shouted aloud. But there is a moment *before* the art. The writer sets out to write with a starting place, square one, we might call it. In the creation text we stand with the Creator in that liminal space, alive, animated, waiting to hear the first words of the novel. How will it begin? How will the Author draw us in? What will be said first? What will the first words be?

My favorite first words in a novel are by John Irving in his book *A Prayer for Owen Meany*. Irving's start captivated me the first instant I read it: "I am doomed to remember a boy with a wrecked voice—not because of his voice, or because he was the smallest person I ever knew, or even because he was the instrument of my mother's death, but because he is the reason I believe in God; I am a Christian because of Owen Meany".[2] What follows is a remarkably human and surprising encounter with brokenness, greatness, drama and God. My first encounter with those words drew me in; I was compelled to turn to page two.

My favorite words in Scripture are the early words of Genesis. They too are captivating, unexpected and the beginning of a story that is yet to be finished: "In the beginning when God created the heavens and the earth, the earth was a formless void and darkness covered the face of the deep." God is known first as a hovering presence who reveals his identity through creative speech: *in the beginning, God.* No one else seems to be present—just God. In the cosmologies of other cultures there is often a pantheon of gods at war with each other and with humankind. There is complexity, violence, conflict, cacophony and dissonance. In Genesis, however, we encounter the imagination and intention of one who has integrity. God is a being of integrity; God has the capacity to make something happen and the agency to do what his imagination and intention will craft. It is a conviction that God is not an idea, concept, myth or abstraction; God is *someone* with whom we must contend. We stand in the moment before and we encounter presence and we hear voice. If the starting place is otherwise, the universe is incoherent. If the starting place is otherwise, God will not move with humankind in the relationality of Trinity.

Spare, irenic, coherent. It is here we meet the speaking presence of the Creator. This is where it all began and begins—with the sound of a voice speaking in time and space. God speaks creation into being. God speaks humankind into being. God speaks a divine-human relationship into being. It starts with God. There was no form and God created form, shape and design. There was a void and God imagined a cosmos filled with nature and humankind. There was no capacity for relationship in speech and God chose otherwise. In the early hours of the sixth day, something is set loose in the universe and a pattern is formed in the divine-human order. God speaks; people have the capacity to respond. God speaks; people are invited to listen—sometimes to echoing thunder, sometimes in the whispering hint of breath, sometimes with words formed and clear, often with something more than words: presence. And sometimes not with words at all. Read aloud and listen to what the poet writes in Psalm 19:

> The heavens are telling the glory of God;
>> and the firmament proclaims his handiwork.
> Day to day pours forth speech,
>> and night to night declares knowledge.
> There is no speech, nor are there words;
>> their voice is not heard;
> Yet their voice goes out through all the earth,
>> and their words to the end of the world. (Psalm 19:1-4)

- God makes earth (time, place)
- God makes language (revelation, culture)
- God makes people (embodied, inspirited)
- God makes community (resurrection, ecclesiology)
- God makes mission (redemption, calling)
- God makes conversation (spirituality)
- God invites relationship (presence, voice)

There is a voice speaking in the world that awaits the response of listening ears. These words assert an alternative life in the world—a life of daring curiosity, of listening to the voice set loose in the world. I fiercely believe there is a way to listen to God's voice in the same way Jesus did as he read Torah. He listened to the voice not only to learn the religious lexicon of Judaism but to enter a conversation. That conversation is what I have come to think of as spirituality. Spirituality is life lived in conversation with another. It is life lived paying attention to the presence of God in all things. Call it biblical spirituality if you must, but spirituality is not essentially religious, and here's the irony— that's precisely what biblical spirituality teaches! Proverbs 9:10 says that knowing God is about wisdom and ordinary, practical insight. So, we must listen to the voice of the God who spoke creation into being. But we do not, many of us. Instead we have learned to silence the thunder of God's speaking voice. Look at how we read Scripture in ways that silence the voice:

- We read cognitively with the mind alone, not to listen.
- We read ideologically to confirm what we believe, not to listen.
- We read informationally for abstract knowledge, not for formation.
- We read critically to seek proof, not to listen.
- We read apologetically for argument, not to listen.
- We read quickly for impressions, not to listen.
- We read devotionally for little bursts of religious feeling, not for encounter.
- We read academically for information, not to listen.
- We read individually for personal gain, not to listen.
- We read literally for answers, not to listen.
- We read objectively, distant from our lives, not to engage another.
- We read conceptually to form worldviews, not for relationship.

Each of these may have value, but they have one thing in common: they lead us away from a posture of expectancy; they keep us detached from readiness to listen for a living voice. We drift away from conversation into something less. The psalmist used even more tactile language, saying, "Taste and see that the LORD is good" (Psalm 34:8). Biblical language is the language of embodied participation, engagement and involvement that leads us to living encounter, to action in response to the voice of Jesus who said, "Follow me. Come with me, go where I go, join me, watch me, and listen." This Hebrew way of knowing God is part of what we've lost—it is grounded, earthy, embodied, sensate, storied and ordinary. It's been said that readers become what they read; I think that's true, but there is something else: readers become *how* they read. "For he [God] spoke, and it came to be." Something happens when we listen in this way. Call it assimilation or metabolizing or revelation; we become formed by the Holy Spirit into the image of Christ. Listening becomes formational. We are formed as we risk what Brennan Manning dramatically and simply called "practical trust": "The faith that animates the Christian community is less a matter of believing in the existence of God than a practical trust in his loving care under whatever pressure. The stakes here are enormous for I have not said in my heart, 'God exists' until I have said, 'I trust you.'"[3]

Spirituality, it turns out, is not something religious but something that starts in a world we can see, touch, taste, smell and hear. God speaks all of the universe into being. Seven days of activity and not a religious thing said, not a religious thing to be found, not a religious anything. God speaks into being sky, earth, water, creatures of all kinds, vegetation and people. Still nothing religious about any of it. God speaks creation into being. A wild landscape filled with what one writer calls "ravished beauty"[4] is formed by the voice of the living one. On the last day of creation, before God takes the first sabbatical, God speaks humankind into being. Life is given. Gender is given. Agency is given. Authority is given. Dominion is given. And notice to whom all of this is given: humankind, male and female. "God blessed and said to them, 'Be fruitful and multiply, and fill the earth and subdue it; and have dominion'" (Genesis 1:28). All of us are asked to care for the newly created universe; humans are given authority and homework to do in the care of our earthly environment. Humans together are asked to listen and enter a living conversation with the Creator.

The implications are clear and dramatic, even stunning! The same voice that created the stars, the moon, the sun, the earth—that same voice is still at work as it was in the first minute of the world, in your life and mine. Theologian Helmut Thielicke said, "I cannot read the story of creation without seeing that I am in it too. In every verse I hear that God is thinking of *me* and that he stopped at no expense to draw me to himself."[5] What God has done, God is doing. God has called us by name on purpose. There is mission to our life. We reflect the image of the God who gives us purpose. It's in our DNA—it's genetic. Barbara Brown Taylor writes of how we find God in creation:

> I know plenty of people who find God most reliably in books, in buildings, and even in other people. I have found God in all of these places too, but the most reliable meeting place for me has always been creation. . . . Where other people see acreage, timber, soil, and river frontage, I see God's body, or at least as much of it as I am able to see. In the only wisdom I have at my disposal, the Creator does not live apart from creation but spans and suffuses it. When I take a breath, God's Holy Spirit enters me.[6]

THE CONTINUING ECHO

The echo of creation begins with God's voice; it continues daily in how we listen. Like all spiritual disciplines, listening requires practice. Jesus did it at home, at meals, on the job, on the road, in the company of friends, alone, in mystical moments and, mostly, in ordinary moments of attention. This speaking voice calls out to us and calls out something *from* us. Listening is not a passive or detached activity done only in mystical solitude; listening is doing what we have been invited and asked to do: care for the earth, honor our relationships, raise up families for the good of others, work hard, make things, love one another and work for the good of those most in need. The prophet Micah declares these words that are hard to ignore: "He [God] has told you, O mortal, what is good" (Micah 6:8). And then, like a good teacher in the classroom, he reviews what has already been told: "And what does the LORD require of you but to do justice, and to love kindness and to walk humbly with your God?" (Micah 6:8). The declaration is sharp: "He has already told you. You know how to live and what to do." Some of what we need to hear is what we have heard already. I remember hearing someone say, "My problem isn't the will of God I don't know yet; it's the will of God I already know but haven't done yet." Listening is also a way of remembering.

FIRST WORDS: A NEW TESTAMENT BOOKEND

Genesis 1 is not the last time we hear about listening in the rhythms of life in Scripture. The beginnings set loose in Genesis find their way into the consciousness of first-century Christians in the writing of John the apostle, probably penned in the last decade of the first century. Almost as a bookend to the Genesis text, John orients his community to listen. First John is a text that is uniquely situated for the majority of people who picked up this book. It was written to Christians who had *some* knowledge of God and faith but now, because of new ideas, new teachers, new information, the certainty of the past was shaken. For many of John's audience, Christianity had become a habit adopted from an earlier generation of parents or grandparents. The tendency was to want to change it—to make it seem more current, more relevant, less demanding. Sometimes following Jesus felt like a burden, something external and something to do, not something to feel or think or believe with passionate conviction. They had borrowed somebody else's faith, and they didn't quite know how to make it their own. Some of them were just going through the motions. It had become hard for them to stand against the world, to deny the things the world habitually allowed itself. And some of them said, "I just don't buy this anymore, I'm going to find a more interesting, more exciting kind of faith or no faith at all." And so they left the church behind, thinking they were moving ahead.

John's Christian community was facing a time of uncertainty about its identity and was getting pretty ragged from it all. Some were getting wobbly because they knew they didn't have it all together. Some felt unsteady in their faith. Some felt their lives were a grave disappointment to God. Some had grown tired, weary and discouraged along the way. And a few believed they had it all together. Then along came John. Tradition says the author of the biblical letters is John the friend of Peter and the one whom Jesus loved. If so, then by this time John is also known as the elder—his is a voice of age, wisdom, maturity, a strong mentor. By the late first century the church of Jesus had been assaulted by people who were leading the church away from the historic faith of the cross of Jesus. So John is the mender who will bring them back to hear the voice of Jesus. He engages a congregation that is in a mess. And he calls them to something dramatic and ordinary. If you want a life that shimmers in the glory of something beautiful, powerful and true, then you want to hear what John will say.

I ask you to read these words *aloud*:

> We declare to you what was from the beginning, what we have heard, what we have seen with our eyes, what we have looked at and touched with our hands, concerning the word of life—this life was revealed, and we have seen it and testify to it, and declare to you the eternal life that was with the Father and was revealed to us—we declare to you what we have seen and heard so that you also may have fellowship with us; and truly our fellowship is with the Father and with his Son Jesus Christ. We are writing these things so that our joy may be complete. (1 John 1:1-4)

As you can see from this prologue, John's interest was in confirming the reality of Christ's work on earth—a huge issue—but the startling irony is that the huge questions were about small things, ordinary things. In the rhythms of their lives something had happened; they had experienced it with ears, eyes and hands. Something was going on in their life, and they paid attention. When they did, they couldn't keep quiet about it. Kathleen Norris, in her book *The Quotidian Mysteries: Laundry, Liturgy, and "Women's Work,"* said that God's attention is given to the small things where we actually live.[7]

John began by stuttering forth a cascade of words about his experience. John's stream of words reflect the wonder that is at the heart of listening. "All good theology begins with wonder." First we listen. And when we do, something happens. Actually, something is always happening, but we are too busy, too noisy and too distracted to hear, see and touch. "Is it an audible voice? I want an audible voice," says my friend Denise. "When do I get the audible voice of God?" I don't know. It's never been an audible voice for me either. But I have heard the voice of God, of that I am sure. The form it takes often changes, but it is most often grounded in that which stands right in front of me. Wendell Berry wrote about Port William, his fictional community, "Port William repaid watching. I was always on the lookout for what would be revealed. Sometimes nothing would be, but sometimes I beheld astonishing sights."[8]

Conation is an academic-sounding wording that I first heard spoken in an Irish accent by my professor Thomas Groome in a class at Boston College. He reclaimed a thousand-year-old way of learning. Cognition is a mental way of knowing, the affective is more an emotional way, and conation is the most experiential way of coming to know. It was what John described in the text above. It's what takes place when the whole person is "actively engaged to consciously know, desire, and do what is most humanizing and life-giving (i.e. 'True') for all."[9] The best synonym, I suppose, is *wisdom*. In wisdom

- we hear.
- we engage in active internal and external dialogue.
- we reflect in constructive engagement with others.
- we act.
- we are changed in these acts of shared praxis.

Listening Requires Intention

Elementary school teachers are learning a great deal about the need to actually teach children *how* to listen. The expectation, obviously, is that children will listen to all sorts of information, analysis, instructions, socialized meaning and ideas. However, classrooms, like the rest of our spaces, are often places of noise, even cacophony, and the noise is both external and internal. One school program offers a four-part process for teaching children how to listen. The strategy is simply called HEAR. The transfer to spiritual listening is obvious.

- **Halt:** Stop whatever else you are doing, end your internal dialogue on other thoughts, and free your mind to pay attention to the person speaking.

- **Engage:** Focus on the speaker. We suggest a physical component, such as turning your head slightly so that your right ear is toward the speaker as a reminder to be engaged solely in listening.

- **Anticipate:** By looking forward to what the speaker has to say, you are acknowledging that you will likely learn something new and interesting, which will enhance your attention.

- **Replay:** Think about what the speaker is saying. Analyze and paraphrase it in your mind or in discussion with the speaker and other classmates. Replaying the information will aid in understanding and remembering what you have learned.[10]

The literacy of spirituality is the literacy of listening. The voice of Yahweh in Torah is insistent, repetitive and clear: "Hear, O Israel . . ." The biblical writers had an instinct for learning how to listen to the internal voice of Spirit, meaning and understanding. But listening is not only a capacity, it is an *intention*. John was not so concerned to explain as he was to *testify*. It has always been thus. In his letters to communities, he repeated these words of participation: "Let anyone who has an ear listen

to what the Spirit is saying to the churches" (Revelation 2:17).
What, then, is our part in spiritual listening? Our part is to stand
around and listen, to look and pay attention, to study, to touch,
to commute, to go to work, to sit at the table, to converse with
friends—to live life with eyes open and ears ready to hear. We
listen and we witness. It begins with God doing something,
saying something, showing something, and in response, we
listen, see, touch and testify in our own voice.

PRACTICE LISTENING: READING SCRIPTURE OUT LOUD

A simple exercise is to read biblical texts out loud—individually,
as a household or with friends. Instead of reading text silently
in your head, practice listening by reading texts out loud as you
might read a story or interesting article for others to share. Read
as the writer might have intended the words to be spoken aloud.

three

HOUSEHOLD

The Stage of the Everyday World

When people want to know more about God, the son of God tells them to pay attention to the lilies of the field and the birds of the air, to women kneading bread and workers lining up for their pay. Whoever wrote this stuff believed that people could learn as much about the ways of God from paying attention to the world as they could from paying attention to scripture.

BARBARA BROWN TAYLOR

BIBLICAL SPIRITUALITY DOESN'T STOP with the first words of creation but continues on the stage of the everyday world. I am not a thespian, but for one shining moment I made a noble attempt. There was a program at my college called New Talents, which gave neophytes an opportunity to experience the opening of the curtain as an actor. In September of my freshman year, I joined a small group of other new talents for a one-act play about something I can no longer remember. I have no answer to why I risked the public embarrassment; I've never been motivated since, but it gave me a love for dramatic recitation that served me well as a teacher and preacher. As the curtain closed on our one and only production, I breathed a deep sigh of relief—I had remembered my lines and didn't walk off the stage at the wrong moments. Still, I can't say I felt any longing to pursue a new life as an actor. A few months after that experience I sat in another theater as truly talented actors drew me in and animated my soul. They took life moments and made them accessible to my mind, emotions and life. I love theater when it is done well.

The word *theater* can conjure up images of great drama, large emotions and epic experiences, but sometimes great theater is crafted around ordinary and universal human experiences: birth, childhood and adolescence, marriage, failure, crisis, emotions high and low, unmet expectations, wild dreams, and unfulfilled hopes. There are moments of high drama and moments of or-dinary, daily life.

THEATER OF GOD'S GLORY

Theater is a powerful metaphor for a spirituality of the ordinary. John Calvin saw the world as a theater of God's glory. It is his language for spirituality. We live in a theater animated by color, energy, song, voice and sound. Seeing life that way changes how we listen for God. The image of the world as a theater insists on engagement: theater is a living, enacted, embodied, visual and verbal experience. We encounter it, are moved by it, repulsed or made angry by it, but we are not passive, not if the script is honest and human. In this theater, God is the lead actor who continues to act and elicit response from the rest of the cast;

something alive and active surges from the stage to the delight, terror, awe, welcome, anger or grief of the rest of the cast. But here's the difference: in God's world we are not only the audience; we are co-creators whose response is made in living moments to the motion, action and voice of the leading actor on the stage. In this theater we *participate* in drama; we listen with heart, soul and mind to narrative; we are present to what is present to us. It began as a theater of created beauty and became a theater of God's continuing movement toward redemption of the now disordered universe. We are not spectators in this kind of theater; the drama draws us in as participants in the moment.

At one point in his writing, Calvin proposed that the church is an orchestra joining the movement on the stage with their own interpretation in sound and song:

> Oceans and mountains provide commanding sets that astound the theatergoers. Trees, birds, and animals serve as a Greek chorus, echoing the theme of God's glory. The audience ranges from humans in general, viewing the production with varying degrees of understanding, to the church down in the orchestra, singing along with the cast. All the while, God is the principal actor on stage, variously arrayed in garments of star-studded fabric, wearing masks that flash the wild beauty of a storm at sea or the calm splendor of an alpine meadow.[1]

Listening is anything but passive. The startle reflex to unexpected sounds is immediate; we jump and turn rapidly to see what just happened. In fact, scientists have now demonstrated that the reflex of listening is faster than the reflex of sight. Sound demands response. Listening is an active response: we show up. Annie Dillard wrote with evocative humor, "Beauty and grace are performed whether or not we will or sense them. The least we can do is try to be there."[2]

There is a pattern in how this works; it isn't mechanical, but it is methodical, rhythmical and repeatable. The subject is God; the focus is on God's already present action in our lives. We listen, or we simply show up; we pay attention. But when you pay attention, you find yourself alive to the next set of questions: *What is God after? What does God intend for my time, my priorities, my gifts, my assets? What is my role in this living theater?* In the beginning, God did not start with the church. God started with a world, a universe, a garden. We should not take that for granted. God is interested in the large dramatic structures of the universe that sustain life and in the most ordinary, small things. The persistent question is, Where does God speak in our lives? Or perhaps it is more accurate to ask, Where does God *not* speak in our lives?

OIKOS: THE STAGE OF YOUR EVERYDAY WORLD

The theater of God's glory is the stage of your everyday world. The show started in the first moments of the creation of the universe, but in the continuing work, after what has been called the eighth day of creation, we became co-creators with God in the care of all that is. *Oikos* is a Greek word that gives us *ecology* and *economy* but basically means "household." Where is that household? Everywhere. "The earth is the LORD's and all that's in it" (Psalm 24:1). When Jacob woke up from a dream reassuring him of God's presence he cried out, "Surely the LORD is in this place—and I did not know it! . . . How awesome is this place! This is none other than the house of God, and this is the gate of heaven" (Genesis 28:16-17). God's interest is in *all* sectors of our household—spiritual, financial, political, social, religious and all human capital. Mary Oliver writes, "Tell me what it is you plan to do with your one wild and precious life."[3] I mean all of your life, the whole of it.

Spirituality is learning to pay attention to the speaking voice of God in everything. That's good news for those of us who live outside monasteries and religious places. Inside the monastery, rhythms are created for listening, often called prayer or contemplation. Seeking God, people go to monasteries and retreats where they are guided to listen. As much as I wish I was a mystic and monastic, I am instead an administrator, educator and president of an organization. I am someone who works in the world of finance, strategic plans, hiring, assessment, meetings and deadlines—hardly an environment for spirituality . . . unless true spirituality is really about learning to listen to *all* that is created.

Biblical spirituality is always grounded in awareness of location. In that sense it is never disembodied but is always grounded in time and place: the houschold, the neighborhood, a local congregation, the family, your workplace, the marketplace, the community. Perhaps that's why good New Testament study is helped by having a map of the ancient Middle East at your side, so you can visualize the location of Capernaum, Bethany, Caesarea Philippi, Jerusalem and Rome, Corinth, Galatia, Philippi, and Ephesus. There is a geography to spirituality because the stage of God's resonant voice is the everyday world. This is not arcane or trivial; biblical spirituality is grounded in sweeping words like *incarnation* (enfleshed), *covenant* (an agreement of relationship between two parties) and *creation*: our lives are immersed in presence and voice. We are shaped by the specific texts of Old and New Testament teachings. As much as we may prefer random texts of our own choosing, the biblical text is given for our formation. We are also shaped by the practice of prayer, which is grounded in both speaking to and listening for the voice of God in the household of our everyday lives.

EARS TO HEAR

On a "spiritual life" retreat with about forty religious leaders and pastors, I was waxing eloquent about early monastic spirituality when I suddenly saw in my imagination the face of my daughter. It wasn't so much a vision as a shocking moment of awareness. At the time she had two small, very active, energetic young boys. In a moment of instantaneous insight I knew—almost nothing I was teaching in that retreat would be possible for her; almost none of it would be available to her in her world of diapers, setting out and putting toys away, preparing lunch and putting it away, working in and outside the home, caring for her family, for others and for her church. The monastic ideal I was teaching that day was fine for monks, but what about my daughter Keri and Jon, her husband, a firefighter? For Bethany the therapist and Kristoffer the commercial banker? For Allison the marketer and Kevin the biotech project manager? Without the luxury of silent retreats, daily spiritual direction and bells for prayer, what is available for the rest of us? For those who live in ordinary places?

Then those words of Jesus echo: "She who has ears to hear, let her hear."

Listening begins with curiosity, a desire to know, to wonder about what is present around us. It begins with longing. Belden Lane says,

> The world dances in wild abandon to an ultimate attraction that it is wholly unable to name. . . . God could have made a bland world in which necessities alone predominate, a mechanistic cosmos stripped of delight and enjoyment.

God might have produced a universe with minimal interaction among all of its parts. But the desire of the Trinity required extravagance, resulting in heaven and earth riddled with desire.[4]

I know some will read these words and conclude this is simplistic, not nuanced enough for reality. Listening is an ordinary capacity, too common to be so powerful. I might even agree but then I remember that Jesus said that anyone who does not receive the kingdom like a little child shall not enter into it. Childlike faith opens the door to this world of dance.

Thomas Merton talked about us taking the world for granted by thinking in what he called "itsy bitsy" ways and said emphatically, "I won't have it. The world is wilder than that in all directions, more dangerous and bitter, more extravagant and bright."[5] Barbara Brown Taylor tells a story of her eyes opening to God's presence after hearing a sermon as a young child:

> My friend's words changed everything for me. I could no longer see myself or the least detail in my life in the same way again. When the service was over that day I walked out of it into a God-enchanted world, where I could not wait to find further clues to heaven on heart. Every leaf, every ant, every shiny rock called out to me—begging to be watched, to be listened to, to be handled and examined. I became a detective of divinity, collecting evidence of God's genius and admiring the tracks left for me to follow.[6]

OUR GOD LURKS EVERYWHERE

What does the presence of God mean for spiritual practices? There is a conversation possible that begins with the living God who calls, speaks into being, whispers a name or nudges one's thoughts. Biblical spirituality always puts it in the same order: God knocks on the door and whatever we do is response. God speaks; first we listen. For many years I took students to the inner city of Chicago for a course on urban sociology and ministry. For eighteen years I heard students speak with eager anticipation, believing that we would bring Jesus to urban neighborhoods. What they discovered, of course, is that God was already there because God walks the streets in time and space. Perhaps Andrew Greeley said it best:

> In Chicago, our God lurks everywhere,
> In the elevated train's husky roar . . .
> A terrifying, troubled, hopeful place . . .
> To be an unclouded light and love and grace.[7]

Our spiritual practices are what we do *in response* to something God has started within. This is not a principle of spirituality; it is the living *relationship* of all spirituality. Our spiritual disciplines are an action not only of human will but also of response to what God has done. We respond to the already active presence of God. It's been said that we cannot create sunlight, but we can do our best to stand in its brightness. Similarly, spirituality is paying attention to God's active presence and seeking to stand in that place. God is alive and revelatory. God spoke in creation and continues to speak into the human story as we listen formatively to God's voice in all of life. That truth changes everything. Is it possible we have silenced the thunder because we no longer participate on this stage of the everyday world?

Practicing a life of listening is already an answer to one of life's most repeated questions, "What is enough?" Listening as a spiritual practice receives whatever comes as gift. Listening as spiritual practice declares gratitude to the One who gives life.

Such words may ring with naiveté in the face of life's pain and battles. It is, however, a defiant faith that battles to remain fully alive to presence and voice in the drama of the ordinary. Perhaps it is fairly simple after all: either we live in the presence of a creative, speaking God or we are alone in the universe. Either we wait expectantly to hear that voice in all of life's moments or we decide there is nothing more God has left to say. Call it faith, call it a contemplative way of life or call it spirituality; whatever term is used biblical spirituality calls us to live fully alive to presence. I'm not an expert at it—I never will be—but I choose to declare there is presence and voice, so I battle to practice awareness and listening. In Latin, the word *absurd* means deafness. I live with a deafness of ear, but I want to defiantly refuse a deafness of heart. By contrast, in Greek the verb *to listen* can also mean "to answer the door," in other words, to give ear to one who is present or entrance to one who waits.

OPENING THE DOOR TO LISTEN

There are practices for listening that can help us open the door to our listening capacity.

Listening consciously. Create practices that prompt you to listen consciously. Just as you intend to turn on your headphones to listen to music, news, sports or other media, so listening consciously is an act of intentionality. *Tuning in* on particular sounds is a physical action. We hear multiple layers of sound every second. Just now I hear the sounds of music being played nearby in the neighborhood. From the back hallway I hear a fan that circulates air through our building. I hear a car drive by in the alley below. Birds chirp a song that tells me the rain will come soon. Voices in conversation float in from a building nearby. Paying attention to the voice I want to hear requires conscious listening. In our age of digital and information overload, listening is a discipline, a literacy to be developed. Seth Horowitz, a neuroscientist at Brown University, calls listening the universal sense. His conclusions about listening in the physical realm are profound for listening in the spiritual realm as well: Listening "tunes our brain to the patterns of our environment faster than any other sense, and paying attention to the nonvisual parts of our world feeds into everything from our intellectual sharpness to our dance skills. . . . The richness of life doesn't lie in the loudness and the beat, but in the timbres and the variations that you discern if you simply pay attention."[8]

Learning to listen as I'm writing about it means we will need to create time and space for listening. In some ancient forms of worship the priest faces the cross and says, "Wisdom." And the congregation responds, "Be attentive." And then again, "Be attentive." And once again, "Be attentive."

Listening mutually. Create practices of listening together. Spiritual listening is the modality of discernment. Discernment means to make meaning out of what we believe we have heard. It is not the practice of problem solving, nor is it primarily about making decisions. It is listening in community. Quakers across the centuries have understood this. They listen together, often in silence, to wait for guidance or truth to emerge. What questions do you ask that invite discernment? I have a friend whose persistent question is, "What do you hear God saying to you in your life right now?" His assumptions are simple: God is alive, God is speaking, and our job is to listen, together. Questions like these may be merely cliché or they may be moments of dramatic resonance. How we are listened to and how we listen is essential. You know when you are "heard" by another because it affects your spirit as well as your mind. You are "seen" by another who can peer into your soul in the way God does—with love, grace and deep respect.

Listening wisely. Create practices for hearing wisdom. Wisdom is a kind of knowing based on experience. Confucius got it right: "By three methods we may learn wisdom: First, by reflection, which is noblest; second, by imitation, which is easiest; and third by experience, which is the bitterest."[9] In wisdom we don't rush to judgment or premature closure. We are patient and wait long enough to hear deeply. In every classroom there are layers of answers from students. Typically the first responses are at a surface level, responses of information or simple reaction. The expert teacher will find ways to ask different or give more time for deeper answers to be formed. Sharon Daloz Parks, a long-time mentor and friend, asks, "What did you hear yourself saying while I was talking?" She understands there is always a conversation going on in our minds—we are hearing but not always listening to the words because our minds are like the CPU on my laptop, processing information in many ways. Listening wisely is making conscious the conversations we have had with experience, insight and discernment. We learn from our experience how to listen and what to listen to.

Listening here and now. The German word for person is *dasein*, literally a "being there," one who is placed or grounded "there." In the school I work at we have a student leadership group called Sacred Space. Their task is to utilize the ordinary space of our building and recognize it as *loca sacra* or "sacred place." Christian faith starts with creation (Genesis 1:1-2), ends in a city (Revelation 22:1-2) and is everywhere touched by the incarnate Jesus, which makes here and now holy, full of grace and presence. Incarnation is God's most audible proclamation that the ordinary is ordinary no more. God always uses the particular for the universal: names, stories, history, genealogies, cities, places, locations, more names, more places. Dorothy Day was right: the more common it is, the more holy it becomes.[10] The biblical list of ordinary things made holy is long: bread, wine, water, flesh, stones, smoke, clouds, ears, eyes, hands, feet, rivers, cities, fields, gardens, corn, trees and children, always children.

It does not mean that we will understand with clarity in all things. Listening well recognizes there are many languages at work at any given moment. A friend of mine is an Anglo who lives in a multicultural neighborhood. Recently a young Mexican American was killed up the street, so my friend attended the funeral mass, which was in Spanish. My friend said, "It's like my relationship with God; I only understood about every ninth word but I knew I was in the presence of something important going on." What changes is the readiness we bring to explore and listen deeply. Living attentive to what we cannot always see or understand changes me from dogmatist to explorer.

Listening also requires that we name the filters that shape what we hear—filters of race, economic status, place, education, gender, sexual orientation, political views and intellectual capacity. All of these shape what and how we hear. We are located in time and place within the limits of our experience, background and genetics. So we can learn to listen all over again as we understand our filters. You say "green" and I hear "red." You say "God" and I conjure up a picture of a violent, cruel and abusive father. You say "faith" and I imagine a mindless flight of fancy, ungrounded in reality. Or I imagine fierce and courageous convictions that led our biblical ancestors to obedience to what they believed was God's call.

I once took coursework at a Catholic university, because I wanted to hear Christian faith spoken in a different accent. At the school I was one of a small minority of Protestants, and certainly the only one raised and ordained a Baptist. I needed to acknowledge the limitations of my filters in order to listen consciously, communally, wisely, and here and now. Just as I needed to speak in different accents of the faith, so my class-mates had to decide how to listen to the Midwest ordained American Baptist. Each week of the program I was paired in shared housing with a Catholic priest. Ironically, my first roommate was Father Church. Our evenings included fasci-nating conversations about words and practices of baptism, the Lord's Supper, preaching, salvation and spiritual formation. The speech was often interrupted with pauses as we stopped to re-define words for each other and tell stories to describe their meaning. When we listen, God's voice will sometimes have a surprisingly human timbre.

For many years I was part of a retreat with student leaders every August before school began. We left the Twin Cities and headed to Red Wing, Minnesota, to the Villa Maria retreat center, run by a group of wonderful Benedictine sisters. One day I went to the chapel to set up for a Communion service. I was busy at my task when one of the sisters hobbled in and asked, "Do you need anything? What can I do to help?" "Nothing, thanks," I said. "I have it all ready. It's all prepared." She smiled, nodded and started to walk out and then turned back and said to me with a wonderful, wise smile on her face and a deep wisdom in her voice, "Well you're correct, the room is prepared, but it was prepared long before you arrived. We've been praying every morning for your time here and the Spirit has been waiting for you." My arrogance was appropriately but gently confronted. What she knew was breathtaking. Preparation starts someplace else:

- in the mind of God the Father
- in the heart of Jesus the Son
- in the movement of the Holy Spirit
- in faithful acts of co-creative listening prayer

You decide: whose voice did I hear that August afternoon?

Paradise Lost

As the narrative of creation continues, paradise is lost, sin becomes the new normal, and hiding and blame are deemed necessary. Belden Lane writes, "The human soul is turned back on itself, twisted by selfishness; nonetheless, God's image remains apparent. Creation, therefore, needs to be revitalized, not destroyed."[11] God isn't surprised or bewildered by the state of our soul; very early on we see God asking questions about the human decision to hide, but then God quickly acts as seamstress, making loin cloths to cover the shame. God doesn't stop speaking once the fall occurs; the voice isn't muted once paradise is lost. God speaks of redemption, work and worship, kinship, family, and community; God speaks in poetry, law, wisdom and prophecy. And God speaks in ordinary things often silenced because we forget to listen. Margaret Guenther instructs students who claim they have little time to pray to find new places and occasions for prayer. "Two of my favorite places are the subway and the kitchen, although both could be seen as spiritually empty.... Directees can be encouraged to pray while walking or before opening a book in the library or while performing manual labor."[12] I do not suggest that listening is easy, only that it is natural and can be learned again if we have forgotten. It is a human ability, available to all, educated and uneducated, rich and poor, young and old.

At the start of the academic year, I sat in a faculty retreat to give an opening word for the year. Before the meeting I walked out behind the building to the Burlington Northern and Amtrak railroad tracks next to our school. I picked up a handful of rocks and brought them to our meeting in a chalice I purchased on the Isle of Iona, in Scotland. Iona is a place of remarkable beauty. Many consider it a place of unique spiritual encounter. With the rocks I wanted to demonstrate the intersection of the ordinary and the spiritual because our work done in the most ordinary ways becomes extraordinary if we remember one thing: the most ordinary things are transformed by the possibility of God's presence. So I gave them each a rock and invited them to put it somewhere as a reminder, a holy relic of the place in which we teach. The stone from the tracks locates us in our place in this time. It grounds us in something ordinary. In the history of religions, we know many religious people thought of the gods as present in nature. The innovation of Jewish spirituality, I believe, was in the sanctification of time—that God is present here and *now*. Abraham Heschel, the brilliant Jewish teacher, called Sabbath "a sanctuary in time."[13] Creation is not the object of our worship; rather, it is a sanctuary of time and space where we stand in the presence of the living God.

PRACTICE LISTENING: KEEP A JOURNAL FOR THE DAY

Place a journal someplace visible as you walk through your day. Keep a record of what you hear and how you heard it during the day. If you are able in your workplace, keep a list of people you talk to, phone calls, coworkers' voices and sounds around you. At the end of the day, ask yourself if you heard the voice of God

during the day and how God's presence was made known to you.
Try this for a week and then stop. Pick it up a week later only if
you find it to be helpful.

four

SURROUNDED BY SOUND

Hebrew Spirituality

*The day of my spiritual awakening was the day
I saw—and knew I saw—all things in
God and God in all things.*

MECHTILD OF MAGDEBURG

THERE ARE SOUNDS WHEREVER WE GO. We hear them
even when we are not aware of listening. Notice the
sounds where you are right now. Listen deeply enough to hear
the many layers of sound that are present.

One type of sound is *white noise*—the humming, whirring,
buzzing and clanking sounds of fans, dishwashers, servers, lawn
mowers, HVAC equipment and machinery we don't even see.
As I walked to my office this morning, I noticed the swishing
sound of the hoses in front of Ivar's Seafood as the workers
power-washed the sidewalk. Further north were the sounds of
waves crashing against the side of the Argosy tour boats. Traffic
was especially noisy on the Highway 99 Viaduct this morning

and then an armada of green and white garbage trucks clambered by rattling and noisy on Alaskan Way.

Another type of noise is *business sounds*—cash registers, espresso machines, dishes clinking and clanking, doors opening and closing, conveyor belts, typing on keyboards, telephones and computers. In the grocery store you hear the sound of shopping carts being pushed into other shopping carts for the next customer, the whirring of the butcher's saw trimming meat for customers and the cashier scanning the bar codes to total your cost.

There are *sounds that trigger emotions*—usually words but sometimes just a tone that triggers feelings of judgment, rejection, frustration or anger. And there are words or tones that trigger contentment and happiness. We all have them: someone sounds like the voice of a parent, teacher, coach, classmate or coworker, and it triggers frustration or happiness, inspiration or guilt, contempt or pride. We have long understood the power music has to create or re-create emotions. Play almost any song by Simon and Garfunkel and I can relive the place I heard it first. Ask me about driving to the north shore out of Boston on a perfect July Saturday as I heard soporano perfection in the tones of Kiri te Kanawa singing "Sanctus," and I am close to tears.

There is another kind of sound as well: *the endless chatter of an inner storyteller.* The storyteller is the voice that speaks in your head to shame you or distract you, confirm you or authorize you, comfort you or implicate you, deceive you or tell you the truth. It is not usually an audible sound, although some days I find myself talking aloud to myself; it is, however, an ongoing inner dialogue. On the ferry the other day a woman talked animatedly on her phone, not seeming to notice that others were able to hear every word: "I will not give in to that voice of shame or judgment or guilt." The storyteller within has been trained by parents, teachers, coaches, enemies, strangers and friends. Our failures have given us ample fodder for the inner storyteller. Our successes are probably not as loud.

There are also *meaning sounds* where you are making sense out of the storyteller in your mind. You hear a familiar song, for example. It may be part of the white noise in a coffee shop, but your brain registers a memory and your internal storyteller begins to narrate the *meaning* the song has for you. Perhaps it was an emotional high point of a memory of love or a turning point when you got a new job or something remarkable happened in a relationship. Perhaps it was an emotional low point when you got the news of an illness or death. Or perhaps it's a sound that simply creates emotion. I walk to my office next to a railroad track on one side and Puget Sound on the other side. There are sounds of a passenger train and ferries and working boats in the harbor. The sound of the foghorn is somehow a comforting sound for me. Trains are a happy sound; I travel contentedly on trains with names like *The Empire Builder, Coast Starlight, Zephyr* and *Lake Shore Limited*. The sound of 118 freight cars filled with corn syrup rumbling through Seattle stirs memories of conveyor belts in factories from my past. Harsh, shrill and sharp sounds of iron on iron take me back to Portable Electric Tools and Swift & Company. Sounds are containers of memory. For some, the ringing of the phone can make them jump in surprise or worry. The many songs and sounds of cell phones, iPads and computers may stir meaning making for us as well. Whatever their source, meaning sounds tend to get our attention.

The apostle Paul talked about listening to our everyday life as a practice that can create transformation.

> So here's what I want you to do, God helping you: Take
> your everyday, ordinary life—your sleeping, eating, going-
> to-work, and walking-around life—and place it before
> God as an offering. Embracing what God does for you is
> the best thing you can do for him. Don't become so well-
> adjusted to your culture that you fit into it without even
> thinking. Instead, fix your attention on God. You'll be
> changed from the inside out. (Romans 12:1-2 *The Message*)

Learning to listen all over again is a spiritual discipline. It starts
with a simple belief that we can train our listening to experience
the voice of God in our everyday, ordinary life and with wonder
about what can happen if we learn another way of listening. In
learning again to listen, we hope Paul is right, that we will be
transformed if we do. Not all hearing is listening, but there is a
way of listening to Scripture that leads to obedience. The New
Testament speaks of hearing "in faith": "We also constantly give
thanks to God for this, that when you received the word of God
that you heard from us, you accepted it not as a human word but
as what it really is, God's word, which is also at work in you
believers" (1 Thessalonians 2:13). Such listening leads to response.

LOSING OUR LISTENING

"We are losing our listening," says Julian Treasure, a student of
sound, speaking and listening. Listening, he says is different
from hearing; listening is "making meaning from sound."[1] He's
speaking of the work of listening to one another in a world that
is increasingly hostile to good listening. In a TED talk he lists
several reasons he believes we are losing our listening skills:

- Something was lost when we learned to record sound; it
  changed listening in relationship to listening in isolation.

- The world is noisy; we have become immune to the cacophony of noise in our world.

- We have traded expansive "soundscapes" for individual sound bubbles of isolated listening by headphone.

- We're impatient with more than the sound bite; listening may require more from us than we are patient enough to give.

- Conversation has been replaced by personal broadcasting (texts, emails and social media).

- We have become desensitized so we require shock and awe to get our attention.

- It is harder to pay attention to the subtle because we are used to the loud.[2]

Of course, he is talking about listening in personal relationships, in business, in conflicts in our culture and world, but he also understands the surprising power of spiritual listening in the ordinary. There is a science to listening that researchers are beginning to study as a discipline of importance. But there is also a spirituality of listening. Listening is making meaning out of sound, and meaning making is a universal human and deeply spiritual instinct. I wonder if we don't silence the thunder of God's voice because we claim to listen for "spiritual meaning" instead of human meaning. Is there a difference? Listening for meaning stirs my curiosity in a world filled with sound. Listening in faith means we listen for the voice of God in the moments and experiences of our day-to-day lives.

I notice that many books on spirituality start with an author sitting in isolation in a beautiful but remote mountain log house, seaside lodge or desert cabin. There's a kind of heroic solitude that erupts into insight and wisdom. I don't reject the experience of those authors, I just don't always know how it helps those of us who don't have the luxury of solitude in our normal location. I remember meeting a professor in New York City who said his best spiritual practice was riding the subway to work. Instead of taking a car with its relative anonymity and solitude, he chose to be where he believed God is revealed most vividly: in the sound of many human voices speaking with distinctive accents and varying timbre, genders, ages and tones—in other words, in the presence of other people in one of the most common experiences shared in North America. He could discern God's presence and voice in his fellow passengers.

DISTILLED IN THE ORDINARY

My commute takes place with about eight hundred of my closest friends, as we say, on the Washington State Ferry. I ride for thirty-five minutes to Colman Dock in Seattle and walk 1.2 miles to my office. I am assaulted by sounds, noise, voices, traffic, machines and the din of a busy waterfront in a busy city. There are times I try to drown out the noise with headphones of the music of Kiri te Kanawa, Sam Cooke or John Coltrane, but more often I practice the discipline of that New York professor—I listen to whatever wisdom is "distilled from the daily."[3]

Where do we look to see God? Where are we likely to hear the sound of God's voice? I live in Seattle, a beautiful part of the world. How can I not be drawn to the beauty of this God when I walk to my office each morning along Alaskan Way on the Seattle waterfront? I can see the Olympic Mountains often shrouded in clouds with a canvas of Puget Sound in the foreground. To the south on days when "the mountain is out" sits the regal 14,410-foot Mount Rainier covered in glacial snow. Even in the clouds and fog it is a place of extraordinary beauty.

On certain glorious days I see an orca or gray whale, Dall's porpoise, and water fowl of unmistakable beauty. I love the beauty of God's creation all around me. The heavens declare the glory of God but so too does the busyness of a port community active with the sound of ferries, cruise ships, tankers, trucks, cranes, fireboats, trains, bicyclists and an entire cast of walking commuters.

It turns out that God speaks in wild and strange ways, in thunderous ways but also in the ordinary in voices we recognize. I write these words in a noisy terminal of the Washington State Ferry. I've decided that will be part of my discipline in this work. I will write in places I inhabit every day, and I will practice what I write. It is noisy today, hard to hear, jammed with many people and sounds, but I wonder, what will be heard if I listen?

In the ancient text *The Cloud of Unknowing*, the writer says, "Be attentive to time and the way you spend it. Nothing is more precious. This is evident when you recall that in one tiny moment heaven may be gained or lost. God, the master of time, never gives the future. He gives only the present, moment by moment."[4]

We live as busy people making choices about time, friendships, work, family and other activities, and we must wrestle with the relevance of spirituality in that space. We are not monastics living in an ordered setting but active people living in settings we must constantly reorder. We are not mystics living apart from neighborhoods, cars, rehearsals, practices, games and evening meetings. We are busy people making choices. "Where does God speak in the rhythm of my life?" is an honest question for us. Do we need to go someplace holy or do something religious? Do we need to schedule time away from family and responsibilities in order to hear God's voice? Do we need specialized training to read in a certain way, pray in a particular form, worship according to a special process and meet God in a shadowy mystical place? How and where do we listen to God? I say start where your day begins. For most of us that is our commute to work.

Hear, O Israel

The *Shema* is one of the most remarkable texts anywhere. It is a section of Torah that contains the core tradition of the Israelites' faith and was repeated twice every day by an entire nation of people as a *mitzvah* (religious commandment). It declares with rock-solid conviction the most profound theological statement ever heard in a world of polytheism. In a culture of many gods, it unashamedly declared the existence of one God. It is a lofty theological text, but it crashes like a glass falling off the counter into a million pieces because it is paired with the most simplistic spirituality ever taught. Read it out loud and listen to the crashing juxtaposition of the divine and human.

> Hear, O Israel: The Lord is our God, the Lord alone. You shall love the Lord your God with all your heart, and with all your soul, and with all your might. Keep these words that I am commanding you today in your heart. Recite them to your children and talk about them when you are at home and when you are away, when you lie down and when you rise. Bind them as a sign on your hand, fix them as an emblem on your forehead, and write them on the doorposts of your house and on your gates. (Deuteronomy 6:4-9)

Hebrew scholars consider this the most important biblical text in existence. At that moment in the religious history of the world, monotheism—one God instead of a pantheon of gods—

was a completely new idea. For ancient Israel this was their spiritual heritage.

- *"The* LORD *is our God, the* LORD *alone."* The monotheism of Israel was a worldview-shattering challenge to the polytheism of their neighboring cultures. In cultures of many gods, Israel had one.

- *"You shall love the* LORD *your God with all your heart, and with all your soul, and with all your might."* In cultures of complexity, there is singular simplicity. Instead of duty, blind obedience and submission, there is love of heart, soul, mind and body—every part of the human identity.

Hebrew spirituality starts with the word "hear"—*Shema* in Hebrew. "Hear, O Israel," it starts, but there is more: *Sh'ma Yis'ra'eil Adonai Eloheinu Adonai echad.* "Hear, Israel, the Lord is our God, the Lord is One."[5] Huge words. Dramatic words. They could make us believe this God is only transcendent, distant, remote, high and lifted up, and somewhere far away from here, from now. But the next words are a conspicuous and sudden crash back down to earth. We hear, "Recite these words to your children," and now the utter simplicity of *Shema* spirituality thunders across centuries of thought: in your heart, at home, with children, when you are away from home, when you lie down, when you rise, in the rhythms of every day and the common routines of the home. Located perhaps in the artwork, symbols and icons that we choose to fix on the walls, doorways and gates of our homes. And wherever we go. In ancient Israel these words were physical, earth-bound reminders of God on their hands, foreheads and tallits (prayer shawls). The people understood that we listen and see when we are reminded in the most ordinary times and places. Talk to your children about these things. Complexity is easy; making complex things simple is not. Teach your children about the deepest things of the universe. It starts as we learn to listen: "Hear, O Israel." These are huge words that shape an entire culture, but they are also small words that shape ordinary experience and daily life.

An entire nation was taught to listen for wonder in the midst of the common moments of their days. Why? Because they knew instinctively that God inhabits those spaces we inhabit. God is a co-resident in our homes. God rides the ferry on my commute. God sits at the table with us. God is present when we lie down, write checks, read our emails, FaceTime our friends, and suffer in guilt, shame and pain. God is transcendent, and still God lives in our homes. Symbols of God's presence are found on hand, head, doorways, houses and gates—all symbolic of entryways to our hearts, minds and souls. They mark ordinary space as sacred space; they infuse common activities with anticipation for something more to erupt in sound, presence or voice. They immerse our days with sacred sound. "Talk about these things." Which things? What you have done, where you have been, what your hands have touched, your mind has thought and your longings have desired. Everything ordinary becomes infused with possibility. Everything becomes a text with revelatory potential. Eugene Peterson is one of those few who can say it with poetry and precision: "The Bible, all of it, is livable; it is the text for living our lives. It reveals a God-created, God-ordered, God-blessed world in which we find ourselves at home and whole."[6]

So an entire culture was shaped by a shockingly simple teaching: Listen where you are. At home, today, now. Brennan Manning told me once in the midst of a very shaky time in my life of faith, "I live in mercy and today." He learned that from

Thomas Merton, who said the world is planted in seeds of God's presence.[7] Today, here, now. An entire lifetime of spiritual practice is compressed in these words: when you are at home, when you are away, when you lie down, when you rise up. They are a primer for the spirituality of the ordinary—learning to listen on the go, on the way, in the quotidian ordinary times of your day. It transforms our life from banal, predictable routine to surprising, sacred pilgrimage. It transforms our worktables into altars for worship and service. And it transforms us all into children seeing a parade for the first time, standing on tiptoes to marvel at the surprising sounds, sights, smells, tastes and touch. Learning to listen in this way enables us to carry out the daily practice Brother Lawrence, a seventeenth-century teacher, called "practicing the presence of Christ." This is the practice of listening for God's voice to come in many voices—familiar voices at home or at work, surprising voices of others along the way and the unexpected voice of God in our own voice as well.

As a Way of Life

I wonder if the Israelites knew there is something notable to the daily practice of paying attention as a way of life, a discipline and a daily practice. They learned to listen to Torah, to Scripture *every day*. In this book I'll frequently discuss the forms spirituality took in Israel's history and the life of Jesus—not only what they taught but how they listened and what containers carried the curriculum. The *Shema* is one example of a practice carried out amid the mundane events of each day. Joan Chittister once said, "Prayer makes us conscious of the presence of God, work makes us co-creators of the Kingdom, holy leisure gives us time for the reflective reading of scripture that makes prayer a real experience rather than the recitation of formulas. Reflective reading of scripture is what draws me into the text and the text into my life."[8]

For Jesus' ancestors, listening was deeply covenantal—a relationship of solidarity between God and humankind set loose in obedient living. The ones who listen to *Shema* are those who love God with heart, soul and strength and seek the good of others through love in the world. To listen is to pay attention and to heed what we hear. A continuing covenant relationship with God created an expectation of commitment to what was heard. It was a covenant with the past but also for the present and future.

Fidelity was not a word I used much until I started to live imaginatively in the world created by Wendell Berry. Fidelity in a community creates what he calls *membership*. Membership is not about a set of rules, although a culture is created that leads to the development of practices and ways of living. In his writing Berry never defines *fidelity*, he just tells stories of people who know they belong to each other, who feel some sense of solidarity with one another and who find ways, even in the midst of their shortcomings and failures, to remind themselves of their commitment to those to whom they belong. They do what needs to be done. There are agreements between them and among them, spoken and not. In the same way, the *Shema* creates a culture of fidelity that defines the "membership."

- *Shema* was kept alive because the Israelites understood it to be a resource for them past, present and future. It was not only a historical curiosity for previous generations but a living word for present generations.

- *Shema* kept faith alive because it required the whole community to understand, interpret and discern not only the occasional "conclusions" but also the questions that point toward those answers.

- *Shema* kept faith alive through covenant, or fidelity, between people and God. Fidelity is about more than blind obedience to commitments; it is about a living partnership of people who are willing to wrestle with the meaning of the *Shema*—not only to interpret what it meant but to be open to a continuing revelation in its words. There is, of course, both receptivity and resistance in every one of us. Today I long to hear the voice of God in *Shema* and Torah, but tomorrow I resist that same voice. Holy listening is paying attention to that which is both receptive and resistant to the voice of God.

Jesus learned his faith in an oral culture, so he literally learned to listen. Scripture was performed, not just read. In the context of a meal, perhaps, the ancient texts of his people were told through visualization, with imagination and different voices. The audience didn't listen passively; they listened by participation, even when the texts were the laws, poetry or teachings. And Jesus experienced listening through what we call collective or social memory; it was not only personal engagement. Jesus listened *in the company of others*. He listened with people he knew; he heard faith spoken in the culture in which he was immersed.

Listening fosters spirituality in its simplest form. Spiritual masters exist, I suppose, but I am suspicious of anyone who doesn't start with the simplicity of *Shema*. Where is God's voice to be heard? Where is God most likely to show up?

- in time (today)
- in space (here and now in the rhythms of daily life)

Listening is a posture of the heart that is willing to be open and to seek meaning, recognizing that the mystery, the holy, is all around. The psalmist asks a question that is singularly haunting in its intensity. "Where can I go from your spirit? Or where can I flee from your presence?" (Psalm 139:7). It's either a trick question or a container of sacred truth. Where can I go that God does not inhabit?

HEARTH, TABLE AND COMMONS

Sharon Daloz Parks says we live and work in three contexts: hearth, table and commons.[9]

The *hearth* represents the most personal places—our homes, family and life as we linger in the intimacy of the daily activities of eating meals, telling stories and completing the work of household economics. In my home the hearth is most often our coffee table.

The *table* signifies places for engagement with others. It moves us outward from intimacy to sharing life with others. Eating together is particularly helpful in building relationships, though certainly not the only way. Neighborhood pubs, workroom tables and conference rooms can all be places for connecting conversations.

Commons are spaces where we work for the larger good. The commons is a global, even virtual, space. What once was the village green in the center of New England towns is now a global space where we seek common grace for the common good. In colonial America, the green was a place for commerce, gossip or news, debate, discourse, relationship, and play. It could provide entertainment by a traveling minstrel or carnival; at other times it was the location for horrific practices like a slave auction and, in some cases, public punishment in the stocks or death by hanging. Symbolic of the marketplaces for economics, law, finance and religion, the commons was a gathering place of local communities apart from the home, schoolhouse, and church or synagogue. Today the commons are those places we work together for the good of all.

SHEMA SPIRITUALITY

Shema spirituality is grounded in the ordinary, embedded in the rhythms of today and tonight. It is practiced at hearth, table and commons, places that represent something universal and natural to our human experience. Jesus frequently called attention to "the seemingly trivial, the small and insignificant—like lost children, lost coins, lost sheep, a mustard seed."[10] God is revealed in ordinary, everyday containers. Pennies, chalk on the sidewalk, conversations with children as you lie down and rise up. Our greatest theologians are often children we love. On Christmas Eve we sat in the back of St. Stevens, a simple stone chapel on Bainbridge Island, with our son, daughter-in-law and three busy little grandsons. Samuel leaned across the pew and asked his grandmother if she knew what happened on Christmas. She told him it was Jesus being born in Bethlehem and then said, "Did you know that Grandma and Grandpa went to Bethlehem?" His eyes glistened with sheer wonder. He stood tall and looked his grandma in the eye with wild anticipation: "Did you see him?"

Wonder in the ordinary.

Holy ground. Listening for God in the voices of children, in the voices of those you know.

Shema spirituality created a change of seismic proportions because it moved the experience of God from religion to all of life. Most of us, Jesus included, spend the majority of our days in the business of work, family and ordinary life. We are citizens of neighborhoods, municipalities, states or provinces, and nations. We are employees who work in offices, factories, clinics, schools, banks, studios and myriad other locations. We are children, siblings, kin, spouses and parents who live in households in homes, condos or apartments. *Shema* spirituality declares that all of these places, identities and relationships belong to Yahweh (God). It insists that spirituality is learning how to live now as citizens of the kingdom of God in what we do every day. For Israel the permanent temple would come later as a symbol of the locatedness of God—"the LORD is in his holy temple, let all the earth keep silence" (Habbakuk 2:20). But in the development of religious life in ancient Israel two things were constant: daily prayer (*Shema*) and the moving tent of God's presence (the tabernacle). Israel understood rhythmic and repeated practices—what could be meaningless ritual or living, sacred encounter. They learned to see God's presence as a moveable feast of God's love.

The tabernacle was symbolic of the place God inhabited in the midst of the people. It was a portable of meeting for God and God's people. "I will dwell among the Israelites, and I will be their God. And they shall know that I am the LORD their God, who brought them out of the land of Egypt that I might dwell among them" (Exodus 29:45-46). With Jesus, the symbolism of the tabernacle becomes a reality. In the New Testament, John writes: "The Word became flesh and made his *dwelling* among us" (John 1:14 NIV). The word *dwelling* is precisely the word used for *tabernacle* in Torah. It means, dramatically, that God inhabited or moved in to the places where God's people live and work. John's Gospel is not the last time the word is used in Scripture. As a forecasting of God's redemption for God's people, John writes in the book of Revelation, "And I heard a loud voice from the throne saying, 'See, the home of God is among mortals. He will dwell with them; they will be his peoples, and God himself will be with them'" (Revelation 21:3). There's a lot of talk about God making God's self at home in places where we live.

Researchers are exploring the human capacity for listening. The science of listening has echoes of the old forms of contemplative listening. Teresa of Àvila called this kind of listening "awareness absorbed and amazed."[11] Origen spoke of "Christ filling the hearing, sight, touch, taste, and every sense."[12] Brother Lawrence called it "the pure, loving gaze that finds God everywhere."[13] Francis de Sales spoke of "the mind's loving, unmixed, permanent attention to the things of God."[14] Each are descriptions of intention, practice and attention. Each speaks of an unhurried and focused awareness.

I'm not much good at contemplative listening, I confess. My writing is aspirational more than actualized. Like many others, I long for something more; I long to hear and sense and know. Like the mountain climber, I am convinced there is something alive as I take the next step on the journey. I love it when I round a turn and find a vista that is breathtaking, a cornice that provides the defining photo of the climb. I am a hiker on the trail eager to mute the buzzing of the deerfly in my face. But I have come to know there is more to be discovered as I pay attention on the journey itself. Here, now, in this moment and in this place. I cannot escape it; there is presence all around me. I'm learning to practice another way of listening.

The sounds around us offer the invitation to listening on the way. Thomas Kelly understands such moments as an entry into the most sacred place of the soul.

Deep within us all there is an amazing inner sanctuary of the soul, a holy place, a Divine Center, a speaking Voice, to which we may continuously return. Eternity is at our hearts, pressing upon our time-torn lives, warming us with intimations of an astounding destiny, calling us home into Itself. Yielding to these persuasions, gladly committing ourselves in body and soul, utterly and completely to the Light within, is the beginning of true life. It is a dynamic center, creative Life that presses to birth within us.[15]

PRACTICE LISTENING: APPROACHES TO ACTIVE LISTENING

Julian Treasure is adamant that we need to teach listening again in schools.[16] He almost sounds like the monastics in their daily disciplines as he proposes five ways to practice listening:

1. Start with three minutes each day in silence, he says, to reset your ears to hear the quiet.

2. Listen to the many sounds, and attend to the particular tones they each have.

3. Savor the music of the mundane.

4. Find different postures for listening—active, expansive and empathetic instead of passive, reductive and critical.

5. Remember the Sanskrit acronym RASA: receive, appreciate, summarize and ask. Receive the sounds you hear, the words, the music and the meaning that you sense in your world. Appreciate—receive with gratitude. Summarizing requires relationships because it is a response to listening; *so* is the word of summary. Finally, ask—clarify, wonder all over again.[17]

five

STORY

Shaped by Biblical Narrative

Listen to your life. See it for the fathomless
mystery it is. In the boredom and pain of it, no less
than in the excitement and gladness: touch, taste, smell your
way to the holy and hidden heart of it, because in the
last analysis all moments are key moments,
and life itself is grace.

FREDERICK BUECHNER

HUMAN IDENTITY IS FORMED and re-formed narratively—
we are who we are as a result of the stories we tell and
retell about ourselves. A few of us write our stories in auto-
biographies, memoirs, journals and novels, but most of us tell
our stories orally to one another. It happens *in vivo* (in life as it
is lived), on the way to something else. Increasingly we tell our
stories in texts, emails and social media in snippets of meaning
or observation. Pictures are attached because they speak a
thousand words. But maturity is the ability to tell and own your

story—knowing and speaking what is true about yourself; the ability to do this directly affects our core human tasks of work and relationship. Further, our Christian identity (individually and collectively) is formed in light of the story of God's action for Israel and in Jesus. The *APA Dictionary of Psychology* defines the self as "an individual's feeling of identity, uniqueness and self-direction."[1]

Stories Matter

Spiritual formation is the process of shaping and retelling our lives within the story of God's action for us. Telling our stories is important, but listening to what we tell in our stories is likewise formational. Listening to your life is the task of reflecting, pondering, wondering and savoring as a lifelong work. It includes reading the impact of family, community, culture, gender, race and place. It is another way to listen for God's voice.

There are actually three stories we tell:

- my story (daily routines of my life and extraordinary, even surprising, moments)

- our story (family, community, networks, "tribe")

- the story of gospel (the unfolding narrative of God's intentions in the world)

All people have a story that needs to be understood and told in order to live into the full potential of our God-given lives. Most of us do not live with a full connection to these stories and have built unhealthy patterns of relating that ultimately keep us trapped and in pain.[2] Dan Allender says, "Our own life is the thing that most influences and shapes our outlook, our tendencies, our choices, and our decisions. It is the force that orients us toward the future and yet we don't give it a second thought, much less a careful examination. It's time to listen to our own story."[3]

Some of these stories are of childhood neglect or abuse, betrayal or even violence. Many stories are more nuanced and haunt us in more subtle but still toxic patterns that play out in our family. All of our lives are marked by evil in some form. As much as we try to protect ourselves and our families from the effects of the fall, we are all bound in harmful patterns that keep us from fully loving God and serving others.[4] In many stories we ended a chapter too soon and concluded that, because of our choices, we were no longer loveable, worthy or good. We came to a premature conclusion about how the story would end instead of listening to the very end. All of our stories are still being written, but many of us have stopped listening, so the unfolding text is lost or silenced.

Stories matter; they are part of our life in conversations, around dinner tables, at offices, and in classrooms, clinics and studios. We tell stories as a way of inviting others into our lives. We live in the stories we remember most. According to science, memories operate selectively but not consciously. We remember in part because we renarrate. We remember in part because some stories will not let us go. But we tell stories to make meaning of our lives. We remember stories of meaning to understand our lives, in the high moments and low. Memory is not a detached mechanism that stores experiences like a thumb drive for a laptop; memory is selective because it is intensely emotional. Try to imagine an unstoried world—it would be flat and boring, one-dimensional, a mere timeline devoid of the richness, color, nuance, humor and humanity stories bring.

Scientists know there are pathways for events and perceptions that travel through neurotransmitters to a part of the brain

where they remain. Formerly, they believed the brain was a file
that stored memory until we called it forward. Today they're less
certain about where the brain holds memory and the role of
things like encoding, retrieval and emotion. But they are clear
that memory resides in our brains *selectively*. And we know that
narratives form memory. A story isn't an exact duplication of the
original event. I know some stories of my childhood only because I remember the telling of those events. Already they have
been interpreted by those who told the story and how I renarrate the meaning to myself. We change in the telling of the
story. The deeper the emotion, the more likely we are to remember the story. It seems more parts of the brain are involved
in a memory tinged with strong emotions. We now know that
memory does not just record, store and retrieve information like
a computer. Instead, our stories shape meaning, order and coherence out of what might otherwise seem to be random episodes. We now know that our stories are a construction on our
search for meaning making. It is not surprising to me, therefore,
that biblical texts are rich with stories told, retold and passed on
to future generations. There is a biblical concept called *paralambano*, which means "to receive something transmitted or
handed down." That which is handed down may be healing or
harmful. We tell our stories to others because we are searching
for wholeness, often in the crush of shattered love.

I had dinner just last night with Zach, a friend whose father
had repeatedly told him a story of devastating destruction
during his childhood: "You are worthless, you will not amount
to anything, your voice is unimportant to anyone except yourself."
His father died on the night before my friend's fortieth birthday.
He had lived in the room of that memory, and the news of his
father's death exploded a dam of anger, shame, hatred and

despair. He was crushed all over again by the memories. In the weeks that followed the funeral, however, something felt different. The voice of his father didn't have the piercing sound of judgment and loathing it once had. The volume was modulated by his father's death, and a year later my friend announced with tears, "This has been the best year of my life. I feel free to be happy. I am, dare I say it, content?" The stories we tell and the stories we listen to shape us.

My colleague Dan Allender goes even further as he declares, "You are a story. You are not merely the possessor and teller of a number of stories; you are a well-written intentional story that is authored by the greatest Writer of all time, and even before time and after time. The weight of those words, if you believe them even for brief snippets of time, can change the trajectory of your life."[5] As you journey through your days and nights, your story is being written—a story of loss, perhaps, as you live in a season of grief or of anticipation as you celebrate the birth of a child, a new job, the conclusion of education, or the birth of a newly developing relationship. It may be a story of pain that is both physical and emotional or of dreariness in a life that seems to roll onward without punctuation points of joy or gladness. Whatever is emerging in your life is a story that is being authored in both conscious and unconscious ways—what some might even call preconscious waiting for the meanings to be made conscious and "heard."

The Biblical Narrative

If the stories we tell and listen to shape our lives, perhaps that's why God's book is full of narratives and, in fact, is itself a narrative that tells a story of creation, fall, redemption and kingdom life. It is the story of shalom, shalom shattered,

shalom sought and shalom restored.[6] Perhaps that's why the
book starts with the author-creator raising his voice to start
the conversation with those created to reflect God's own image.
Perhaps that's why humankind's early words included words
of blame, scapegoating, rebellion and hiding. But there is
something more that stories create in the very form they take.
Stories are concrete, grounded, embodied and particular. Ideas
can be conceptual, theoretical, general and fanciful. They have
power; of that I am sure. But the power in stories is in their
particularity; stories have edges and boundaries in the characters, plot, time and space.

Christian spirituality is grounded in gospel, good news an-
nouncements that God has shown up in the particularity of one
man, a first-century, bilingual, dark-skinned, religious Jew born
into a family that soon became a single-parent family; this
family had been political refugees as they escaped persecution
from a king named Herod and returned to a small town in
northern Galilee. Jesus worked as a carpenter in another town,
practiced the religion of his culture and later was sought out as
a teacher. That's where the trouble begins. Jesus is not an abstraction; Jesus' story keeps spirituality from becoming an exercise in imagination where we create God into whatever image
we choose. The particularity of story keeps us from customizing
God and keeps us focused on the unfolding drama of God's
movement in our life. We silence biblical narratives when we
homogenize them to "principles" of life and sermon illustrations
instead of listening to the particularity of each person as they
lived in time, place and culture. Too quickly we skip past the
details on a manic search for "truth," when truth is often found
in those details. Jesus was a bilingual Jew who worked as a carpenter and rabbi in the early years of the first century. Paul was

an urban Jew trained in Jerusalem by the finest teacher of the day who lived as a Roman citizen and as a tent-maker apostle who traveled the entire Roman world. Luke was a physician, Peter a fisherman, Dorcas a businesswoman, Priscilla a teacher and Timothy a young mentee and pastor in training. None of these are abstractions, principles or "models" as much as they are a story to be read.

Listening to your own story seems to be especially important in times of medical crisis, long-term medical treatment and terminal illness. Difficult or scary life experiences can drive us to listen with urgency for meaning, hope or comfort. Is that because we find ourselves compelled to slow down, listen differently and pay attention? Medical research is thick with studies, theories and debate about how spirituality, religiosity and health interact. A single definitive conclusion will never have unanimous support in the medical community, but the questions themselves continue to raise the very theme of this book: something more is going on in our lives than can be explained by the merely physical. Biblical spirituality tenaciously sticks to the claim that God is alive, active and at work in the unfolding realities of our stories. Listening is our own act of tenacious openness that we might discover how this is true in the particular moments of our lives.

Listening to biblical narratives helps us become skilled in listening to our own narratives. As we listen for God's voice in biblical texts we learn to listen for God's voice in our own stories. It is active listening, a skill to be practiced. What was the place of storytelling in your home? If it happened in your household, where did it take place? The kitchen table is one such place for me—a time for good food, for jokes, teasing and laughter, learning together and listening to the stories of our own lives.

We asked, "What happened today?" "How did it go?" "What do
we need to know about the day?" When our own children were
very young, our bedroom was another gathering place for stories
to be told. The kids piled in and soon there were five of us on a
king-size bed laughing, teasing and telling the stories of our life
to each other. When grandchild number one came along, that
practice included storytelling with Benjamin. He stood at the
foot of our bed and made up stories on the spot for us. They were
mercifully short, always funny in a two-year-old sort of humor
and formulaic: they always started with the words "One upon a
time." (That's not a typo, just a two-year-old's version.)

Narratives are profound on their own; I find them devastat-
ingly more powerful when I hear them spoken in the voice of
the author. So, I listen in novels for the voice of the one who
crafted the words. On occasion, I listen to audiobooks read by
authors because of the distinctive inflections and meaning they
give as they read sentences they themselves crafted. I remember
the day I heard words from Frederick Buechner that caused a
seismic shift in my thinking about all of this: "All theology, like
all fiction, is at its heart autobiography."[7] That shifted the tec-
tonic plates in my mind, but he didn't stop there. "It seemed to
me then, and seems to me still, that if God speaks to us all in
this world, if God speaks anywhere, it is into our personal lives
that he speaks."[8] When I heard the meaning of those words, I
knew: life then becomes a holy narrative. The word "biography"
comes from the root of two words: *bios* and *graphia*. It means
"that which is written on your living cells." It is holy because
God is intimately involved in the writing of the story of your
life. It is life embodied, incarnated in the rhythms of days and
nights. Listening for the voice of God is something we do by
narrating the meaning we make of our lives. It is a dual process

of listening: we listen for the meaning in our lives and someone listens to us tell the story in a way that can help us hear even more deeply.

CHANGING HIS STORY

Jacob's story is one that I am drawn to often. Jacob was the second born in his family, a twin to brother Esau. The story of his birth is a visual of the narrative that is to come: he was born clinging to the heel of his older brother. As a child I believed he was one of the great heroes of faith; perhaps he is, but his name tells a shadow part of his story. The name Jacob means supplanter, which is precisely what he did. When his time came as a young adult, he defrauded his father and stole his brother's birthright to the family estate in a deliberate attempt to supplant his brother's place of power and authority in the family. Not surprisingly, Esau's response was anger and revenge; he threatened to kill Jacob after their father's funeral. So Jacob took off running and, in a classic story of avoidance, went into hiding and turned to God in a kind of vending machine prayer in which he asked God to save him in exchange for giving a tenth of all of his assets to God (Genesis 28:20-22). As if God could be bought for a tithe, Jacob again followed his childhood identity, this time intending to supplant the place of God.

More like something out of a pulp fiction novel than a biblical text for teaching, preaching and spiritual guidance, this is a story remembered by the community of Israel and told as part of the living legacy of their national story. Remarkable. Raw and honest about human wickedness, deception and abuse, the narratives of Scripture are a portal into listening to all of your life. We listen to such stories not to emulate the best virtues of the characters and not to study religious truth; we listen to such

stories to pay attention to where God can be heard and seen. We
listen to biblical narratives because they prod us or elbow us to
pay attention. The questions we want to ask Jacob are perhaps
the very questions we ask of our own story. We might want to
say, "Jacob, your foolishness is conspicuous and your arrogance
is unmistakable. Did you think you could get away with it all?"
"What kept you from living in the generosity and grace of God?"
"Did you know you were being shaped by both the pain you felt
and the pain you caused?"

Several years ago, I was preaching a sermon on God as creative artist, God as the potter who shapes us as does the artist
working with malleable clay. I asked one of our potters on
campus, an outstanding artist, to bring in a potter's wheel and
work the clay as I preached about God's presence and work in
the artistry of our lives. Of course, from the very beginning,
not one single person looked back at the pulpit once the spot-
light shone on Kirk and his wheel. Most people told me later
they were mesmerized by watching his hands work the clay,
shaping, forming and molding. I could see nothing of the audience, but at one point there was an audible gasp from the
whole group when a beautiful, tall pot had taken shape before
their very eyes. It looked like Kirk was going to spend the rest
of the time finishing, refining and adding artistic touches to
his pot, but suddenly he took both hands and held them over
the pot, wheel spinning, and flattened the tall shape, returning
it to a lump of clay spinning on the wheel. Ten minutes later
a large, softly rounded pot emerged, even more beautiful than
the one before. The clay had little say in the work of the potter
except to submit to its emerging shape, to accept what the
potter was intending for it. The clay, formed of products of the
earth, is not the potter. Interestingly, the word *humility* has its

roots in an ancient word for soil—grounded in the very earth to which we will one day return.

In time Jacob learned that too. Twenty years later he decided it was time to go home. He came, in fact, to the same riverbed where he had stood and prayed before. Again he was filled with fear. Again he had reason to be afraid. Again he was heading into an uncharted part of his life and that filled him with anxiety. Twenty years before he was running *away from* his brother. This time he was running head on *into* Esau and his army of four hundred men.

And again he prayed. But this time his prayer was different. In Genesis 32 we read,

> O God of my father Abraham and God of my father Isaac, O Lord who said to me, "Return to your country and to your kindred, and I will do you good," I am not worthy of the least of all the steadfast love and all the faithfulness that you have shown to your servant, for with only my staff I crossed this Jordan; and now I have become two companies. Deliver me, please, from the hand of my brother, from the hand of Esau, for I am afraid of him; he may come and kill us all, the mothers with the children. (32:9-11)

This time there is depth and maturity in his prayer. There are no deals or bargains offered to God. Instead there is a spirit of humility. There is wonder at God's mercy. There is recognition of his own unworthiness and sinfulness. There is honesty given to the feelings of fear that fill Jacob's heart. In essence he prays, "God, I have no claims on you and nothing to offer you. You have already given me more than I had any right to expect. There is only one reason for my turning to you now—because I need you. I am scared; I have to face up to something hard tomorrow, and I am not sure I can do it alone." This time he doesn't ask God to make Esau go away, magically erasing the wrong he has done to his brother. He doesn't ask God to ignore his sin and the need for reconciliation. He doesn't ask God to take away all of his troubles and miraculously rescue him. Instead he asks— what we can always ask—that God will help him to face his troubles so he won't have to face them alone. Perhaps the story is told for that reason as well as to describe the lineage of Jesus. In time, Jacob's name (supplanter) is changed to Israel, the one who contends or wrestles and strives with God. And God remains present to this one whose name could just as well have been "deception." Perhaps what can be heard is the whisper that God's name—mercy, long-suffering, grace and love—is the name to know.

Sanctified Imagination

Unless we hear the stories of the Bible as our own stories, as stories about us, we silence the text and don't truly hear the Bible at all. Biblical narratives reveal, resonate with and invoke response as we listen to them as conversations with God about ourselves. In what we might call sanctified imagination, we discover we are not reading Scripture as the history of someone else; we are reading scripts in which we ourselves are in on the action. We are listening. We are engaged. We know this story is somehow the story of our own participation with God. When we listen in that way we narrow the distance from God and allow the voice to be heard within. Abstraction is the enemy of listening to God. God seems always to be interested in inviting us into the action, but not as heroes or celebrities. Instead we are participants. As Jacob deceived I am invited into my own deception. But I'm not merely invited into a morality play:

"Don't be a supplanter like Jacob or a fool like Esau." Rather, it is a way of listening to my life where God has something to say to me. When I say that listening to biblical narrative requires the practice of sanctified imagination I mean I must imagine myself in the story in a place of conversation, confrontation or confession; I may be desperate for grace and seeking redemption or just a "welcome home." I may be on the run from my family, wrestling with God or hiding as a consequence of my choices. I may be in flight and evading my own fear. I may be all of these or more, but one thing I am not: an idle bystander.

We develop the ability to listen by reading biblical narrative and the entire Bible as sacred conversation. God is present in Torah and poetry, in instruction and psalm, prophetic writings and unfolding history as we listen for the voice of the living God. It is no wonder *lectio divina* was one way early Christians read Scripture. *Lectio divina* is the practice of reading the text listening for what God is speaking into your life. It is a way of reading by standing in the presence and hearing the speaking voice in my life. Those early readers didn't succumb to the trap of reading for information alone; they read in expectation of revelation in the present moment. I know some fear that such a way of reading might reduce Scripture to an individual's mystical experience rather than to exegetical truth, but in the same way a sermon is an attempt to hear the voice of God for this ordinary life, listening with sanctified imagination *engages* truth. Truth is not handed down in direct, didactic revelation; it is always translated and interpreted.

Earthy spirituality it is. I use that term because, for me, it describes the truest forms of spirituality that I know—honest, human spirituality. This may be why we need to read story with our ears. I have spent a lot of my life trying to live as if I were

God or one of those so-called heroes of faith, as if my faith
was always strong, as if I knew the answers to all of the questions, as if I even knew all of the questions. But God doesn't
ask that we rise above all of life's pain; rather, he asks that we
bring all of our story to God. God doesn't ask that we walk
around in disguise pretending there are no holes in our hearts;
God asks only that we bring those painful hearts to the throne
of grace. *Bios* and *graphia*: what is written on the living cells of
your life, your story, your unfolding experience with God? Another way to think about that question is to wonder about the
process of memory.

STORY AND MEMORY

Memory begins with perception—you hear or smell or see
something and you pay attention to it. Those perceptions find
their way to the hippocampus in the brain, which probably sorts
out various data to decide what will be kept. Here the science is
less clear. The information moves from perception to hippocampus to nerve cells to synapses, which release neurotransmitters to dendrites. But something happens as we try to make
sense out of memories through the telling of our stories.
Whether we hear or remember something precisely as it was is
not so important; the important piece is that something happened that caused us to pay attention. Science isn't very clear
about what captures our attention in the first place, but it understands that something "called out to us" and got us to listen
in the first place.

It is also fascinating that there are multiple types of memory,
beyond just short-term and long-term. In the science of seeking
to understand the brain and memory, researchers seem to speak
of at least five forms of memory.

- There is memory of specific facts and information, sometimes called *declarative memory*. You remember your mother's maiden name and your father's date of birth. You remember where you went to school in grade one. This is sometimes also called autobiographical memory because it consists of stories from your own life.

- There is memory of events, sometimes called *episodic memory*. When you were six you wandered off to the vacant lot near 108th Street and your friend's Daisy air rifle was taken by another group of boys also playing where they should not have been.

- There is a basic memory of how to do things repeatedly—you remember how to drive the car, how to get home and how to type. This is *procedural memory*.

- *Spatial memory* is a type of memory about the place you live, the environment, including landmarks in your location.

- The memory that is most curious to me is *semantic memory*— the memory of concepts you've learned and of meaning given to events, people and experiences in your life. What makes it most profound is that it requires the work of interpretation, of making meaning out of facts, events, episodes and stories, that is, out of the unfolding of your life.

It's been said, "The entire Torah may be summarized in one word: remember." Remember facts, life events, places, procedures of life and worship, meanings, and the map of life you carry in your head. But, most of all, remember, Israel, you have a story with God. Remember that you once were slaves in Egypt. Remember God delivered you. There is meaning and movement in our lives. Each story is not a solo episode that exists in a vacuum but is somehow connected with what has gone before. The ancient church spoke of a great cloud of witnesses; they were aware that our lives are not lived solo but that we are part of the dream and experience others had before us.

"God often shows up disguised as your life," someone said.[9] Richard Rohr takes us further: "We belong to a Mystery far grander than our little selves and our little time. Great storytellers and spiritual teachers always know this."[10] Making meaning out of our lives is not simply reciting facts or repeating events but seeing interconnection and intersections and finding coherence in the seemingly random moments. If Rohr's words have any ring of truth to them, it changes how we listen. If there is Mystery in the presence of God in my life, then I know that God is speaking through everything. When someone says thank you for something you have done, it is a gift of gratitude from God. When someone shows you love, that love is a gift of grace from God. When someone tells you the truth, it is a gift of love because God cares to move you from your defenses, hiding and resistance. Telling our story to one another is perhaps the most sacred thing we do because God shows up in the words, emotions and crafting of our words.

Oddly enough, the stories of the "great heroes" of biblical faith are often stories of crisis, abuse, trauma, shame, lust, greed, oppression, failure and abandonment. Few are heroes of their own stories, so why didn't someone clean up the Bible and edit out the bad stuff? Because they wouldn't be gritty, honest or a true reflection of the human experience. I remember listening to a wise spiritual teacher answer the question "What is the best spiritual reading you do these days?" "I read novels," he said simply. He knows that novels explore all parts of the human condition. Novels are stories of our attempts, successfully or not, of being human—like the narratives of the Bible itself.

In his book about the life of David, Eugene Peterson won't let us off the hook:

We can't get away from God; he's there whether we like it or not, whether we know it or not. We can refuse to participate in God; we can act as if God weren't our designer, provider, and covenant presence. But when we refuse, we're less; our essential humanity is less. Our lives are diminished and impoverished.[11]

Sometimes I pray and listen for clarity; what I often seem to get in response is silence. So I pray for meaning; what I often seem to get is just more of today, tonight and tomorrow—work, meals, sleep, colleagues, friends, family and routines. Where is God supposed to be in that? Wendy, my wife, lives with chronic pain—daily suffering in the joints and nerves from idiopathic neuropathy. She often spends her day trying to calm the pain. Where is God supposed to be in that? I long for the audible voice but live instead with the unfolding story of my life, sometimes with faith and sometimes without.

Recently a twenty-six-year-old man walked onto the Seattle Pacific University campus near our school with a shotgun. Almost forty rounds were fired before a heroic young student took the gunman to the ground and subdued him with pepper spray as others joined him in holding the gunman on the ground until the police came. Tragedy and heroism are part of all of our stories.

LISTENING TO YOUR STORY

Listening to your story is a lot like learning to read a novel. You look for the plot and for themes that seem incoherent or random but might lead to something important. New characters are introduced, and you puzzle over why they appeared at that particular moment. What does it mean? Old characters are developed; you see more and more of their depth in the nuances of unfolding conversations. You learn to listen to the accent of their voice in their individual presence in the story and also the blind spots, ignorance, even their failure to recognize their part in the drama that is unfolding. Book clubs have become a kind of cottage industry these days. People gather to read books together and tell each other what they heard, saw, learned and didn't see. Often they listen to others and discover a clue they missed that someone else noticed.

And yes, there is danger in over-interpretation. The writer who is most important to me, Wendell Berry, is apparently unimpressed when we jump too quickly to interpreting meaning. The front page of his novel issues this warning.

Notice

Persons attempting to find a "text" in this book will be prosecuted; persons attempting to find a "subtext" in it will be banished; persons attempting to explain, interpret, explicate, analyze, deconstruct or otherwise "understand" it will be exiled to a desert island only in the company of other explainers.

BY ORDER OF THE AUTHOR[12]

So maybe we should keep listening. Maybe meaning making isn't a finished product as much as a true Torah, a way of life. Maybe listening isn't a simple physical capacity but a way of life. Do you see how that changes everything? Listening is not a religious practice; it is a normal human practice in the "thickness" of life. There is no formula for this; we listen to our own lives, in moments of great apparent drama and weight but also in moments that seem as routine and ordinary as my Cheerios at breakfast.

My first spiritual director, Gloria McClanen, was both wise and smart. She started our work together each time with three questions:

- What were the highs of the week?
- What were the lows of the week?
- How faithful were you to the disciplines to which you committed yourself?

It seemed her intent was to ground our work together in the unfolding story of my life. Brennan Manning, who was also wise and smart, told me that the most important spiritual practice is to show up. For Gloria that meant listening to the highs and lows of my week. Why? To help me learn to listen all over again. To train my ears and eyes to listen to my life. To teach me to listen to my own life, *as I live it*, not as I imagine it should be. That's not a strength of mine. I am a Scandinavian male who prefers control, answers and technical protocol to something as vague as "listen to your life." I prefer to be given principles that are abstracted from someone else's life to apply to the work of listening to what God is doing in mine. Unfortunately for me, it turns out, God inhabits my life differently than he inhabits others' lives.

How do we make meaning? We are, it appears, continually composing a relationship with our own stories. Stories are not simply the words, arrangement, and movement of plot and interaction of characters. Stories take on a life of their own in our telling and retelling of them. One of our signature programs at The Seattle School is simply called Story Workshop. Participants are asked to prepare a written narrative, a slice of their story to be read in a group of people they have yet to meet. When they gather in Seattle or Chapel Hill, Dallas or Virginia, they read the story aloud so that others will . . . will what? You see, that's the question. I asked our team why they take the time to read the stories aloud. Couldn't we economize by just writing them out so that others can read them? The answer given was unexpected: "Because that's the transforming moment. People are changed as their stories are heard." We're studying hard to try to understand why this happens, but we know it to be true. People carefully craft and pen their stories, poring over words, sentences and paragraphs. They sweat and suffer to get the words just right. They agonize over their experiences of betrayal and delight. And when the moment for the listening comes, they are emotionally on fire—alive, alert, waiting. It is a moment of panic for some, relief for many, redemption for a few and transformation for all. Something happens when I tell my story aloud for you to listen. It doesn't always matter what stories we tell but biblical narratives give us a hint.

"Stories show us how to bear the unbearable, approach the unapproachable, conceive the inconceivable. Stories provide meaning, texture, layers and layers of truth."[13] Those are the words of a horror and dark fantasy novelist. She might have read the psalms. Their spirituality is not an invitation to story-telling as much as a necessity to tell stories. Life happens to us in a series of unrelenting moments of high points, low points and turning points, and we are shoved to the edge of a cliff, compelled by life itself to become storytellers. We don't *want* to tell our stories as much as we *need* to. We need story and poetry to show us how to bear the unbearable, approach the unapproachable and conceive the inconceivable. Think about it. If the function of an organism is to organize, the function of humans is to organize meaning. We are compelled toward coherence. We are pushed by life to make sense out of the senseless. So we learn to be storytellers. Unlike novelists who might choose the characters and plot, life is its own unfolding story. We don't narrate it from a distance but up close as it unfurls.

Telling your story is not a cure or remedy for sin, but it offers a way to understand what holds us back from being able to love and be loved and gives us the capacity to see and live into our calling. We must be able to tell our stories with integrity and listen to another's story with care, empathy and skill. These things are learned by telling our story in a setting where others can help us read the themes present and offer clarity and vision. Of course, this is all predicated upon the idea that our unintegrated narratives are usually our tragic stories that have resulted in ambivalence, powerlessness, betrayal, contempt, shame and indifference. Regardless of how we choose to protect our broken hearts, these structures keep us separated from the full potential of relationships, including the way we relate to God. They are strongholds that bind us to our trauma and keep us from true delight and the goodness of living and leading in the kingdom.[14]

THE RESONANT SOUND OF SILENCE

We cannot hear if we are never silent, never still. We can only hear God in the noise of life if we learn to hear God in the silence of life. Paul Simon wrote a song that still stirs me though I heard it first as a young college student. He spoke of the "sounds of silence," a seemingly contradictory collection of words.

Spiritual directors consistently encourage exercises and disciplines of silence.

- Silent prayer: no words, just listening.

- Silent reflection: listen and write what you hear in the stillness.

- Technology sabbath: turn off anything that requires technology and listen to what else is present.

- *Lectio divina*: read Scripture or other texts not to master content but to discern God's voice or God's stillness in short, focused reading of text.

"Be still, and know that I am God" (Psalm 46:10) is a word that is counter to the culture of sound, noise and distractions that compete for our attention. It is also a word of spiritual practice as necessary as water and oxygen. I once spent an entire day in silence because it took me that long to find a quiet place for listening. Fueled by adrenaline and busyness, I have to be intentional about creating a free and open space where I can listen. The words "be still, and know that I am God" challenge how I live and the intensity of my personality, work style and nature. T. S. Eliot asked the question in his poem "Ash Wednesday," "Where shall the word be found, where will the word Resound?" His answer is haunting: "Not here, there is not enough silence."[15]

What is the purpose of silence? Howard Thurman wrote, "The true purpose of all spiritual disciplines is to clear away whatever may block our awareness of that which is God in us. The aim is to get rid of whatever may so distract the mind and encumber the life that we function without this awareness."[16]

PRACTICE LISTENING: LEARNING TO READ

There are many different ways to read a story. If it's a novel, we might read it one way with certain expectations for entertainment, mystery or drama; if it's a newspaper, we will read in a different way. Use the following list of suggestions as a guide for a variety of ways to reflect and "read" the unfolding story of your life.

1. Read like a reporter looking for descriptions of facts (what is heard, seen, tasted, touched and smelled). Look first at the details of what is told.

2. Read like an artist looking at the imagery in words chosen to describe events and figures of speech, especially similes, and metaphors to describe what the events felt like to the writer. Look for hints or whispers of God's voice in your life today.

3. Read like an excgete, trying out different interpretations as you speculate about possible meanings. What might this event mean for the larger plot? Is this a defining moment? Look for the beginning of meaning in recent events in your life.

4. Read like a geographer for location and point of view. Where you stand changes what you see. What biases, blind spots or worldviews are at work in the story? Look to see how your perspective affects how you feel about events in your life.

5. Read like an English teacher to study syntax, patterns of grammar and the formation of words. What patterns are repeated? What changes in the tone of the book? Who is speaking? When? Why? What words seem important? Are there words that trigger emotions of anger, sadness, shame, joy or longing? Look for patterns, characters, tone and triggers. Look especially to see whose voice is loud in your narrative right now.

6. Read like a classmate in a learning community where others will join you in asking great questions about what is written.

What do the questions of others provoke for your own meaning making? What do they see in your story that you cannot see without the vision of others? Listen to what others are telling you, especially if their perspective gives a very different meaning than your own.

7. Read like a writer looking for humor, irony, the juxtaposition of themes, tragedy, comedy and myth. Are there themes that repeat themselves that seem important?

8. Read like a librarian looking for information, formation, transformation, literature, comedy, tragedy, history and science. Look for all that makes life fascinating.

9. Read like a reader: just keep on reading. Before you bring closure to the meaning of a story, read it again. Read to savor the moments. What is especially enchanting in your story at present?

This process doesn't always leave us with clarity and insight, but I'm not sure I want to live all of my life without mystery and the unknown. The apostle Paul once said, "For now we see in a mirror, dimly, but then we will see face to face. Now I know only in part; then I will know fully, even as I have been fully known" (1 Corinthians 13:12).

six

TRAJECTORIES

Oriented by the Psalms

*The spiritual life does not remove us from
the world but leads us deeper into it.*

HENRI J. M. NOUWEN

SOMEONE SAID TO ME RECENTLY, "My life is a jumble of surprises, twists and turns. Nothing seems nailed down. I don't know what's coming next." He had earned the right to such words because in the space of two years he had lost a job, replaced it with another, met the woman he would later marry, moved twenty-five-hundred miles to a new home, and left a spiritual director, church and familiar community where he had lived for a decade. His life was in such high speed he wasn't sure he could keep up with all of its dizzying motion. Disorientation was an almost weekly experience for him. He wasn't a monk, nor was his a monastic spirituality based on lifelong vows of stability, commitment and predictability.

Most of us are not monastics able to fashion such a life; ours
is a life familiar instead with transitions, changes and surprise. I
suspect that's why religious traditions over the centuries have
centered life in a group of poems known as the Psalms. They
seem to have one unifying purpose: to free us from the illusion
that life is easy and orient us to live into whatever comes. Many
of these poems are what we call wisdom writings, which also
have a unifying theme: to tell us the truth, to give us an account
of the way life actually is. Novelist Flannery O'Connor said
what I think Jesus heard in the Psalms: "You have to cherish the
world at the same time that you struggle to endure it."[1] There is
a product line that proudly declares "Life is good" on T-shirts,
mugs and jackets. But we all know better: life is also hard. I want
life to be good, but I do not live naive to the tension of struggle.
Don't give me bumper sticker spirituality because it can't keep
up with the reality of life as most of us live it. We need something authentic, gritty and honest, writing filled with resiliency,
anger, hope, joy, wonder and struggle against the headwinds of
life. The Psalms give us all of that. In fact, John Calvin called
these poems "the anatomy of all parts of the soul." They offer a
glimpse of what we could also call an anatomy of faith. I think
that is why some of us are drawn to their awful honesty: we long
to know how the soul works, even though these poems don't
make it sound easy. How we listen and respond to all parts of
our stories takes hard work, and we often need spiritual com-
panionship in seasons of storm and disjuncture as well as seasons
of sunshine and equilibrium.

ORIENTATIONS

It was Walter Brueggemann whose pragmatic typology of the
Psalms gave me the most truthful way to listen to even the most

difficult parts of life. His study of the forms in which the Psalms were written concluded there are three broad forms in which they functioned in the life of their first listeners. There are psalms of orientation, disorientation and new orientation.[2]

- *Psalms of orientation* are like the "Life is good" bumper stickers I see on Bainbridge Island. They include psalms of creation, wisdom and blessing. Life is organized and orderly, offering simple choices to walk in the way of godliness or not and reliable obedience. There aren't surprises. For examples of these, read Psalms 1, 127 and 133.

- *Psalms of disorientation* are like the bumper stickers that say, "s___ happens." Life is experienced as disoriented with displacement as the new normal. These are individual and communal psalms of lament, suffering and pain. There are surprises, and the news is not good. Read Psalms 42 and 88 for an example of these.

- *Psalms of new orientation* don't seem to have a bumper sticker. They're more like the T-shirts sold at our local ice cream store that say "Life deserves extraordinary." These psalms are songs of surprise, awe and celebration: life has been restored, redeemed or released into a new possibility. There are surprises that cause us to break into thanksgiving and evoke celebration. Psalms 30, 34, 124 and 150 are examples of psalms of new orientation.

In my life, there is movement, dissonance, right turns followed by collisions, which require left turns, and the uncertainty of travel without a map. There is no GPS given for life; the Psalms are a loudspeaker declaring the Bible does not provide a turn-by-turn outline for this journey. There are trajectories oriented by careful reading of biblical texts, particularly the Psalms. But there is no road map given to guide you with clear, simple directions. Instead the Psalms insist on something else: paying attention to all of your life and to the hints of God's presence in sometimes dramatically changing circumstances. Did God change or become silent in the middle of those circumstances? In one season it felt like God is reliable, in charge, consistent and present; the earth is the Lord's and life just simply works. Best of all, it all makes sense. But then collapse may follow, and we cry with Jesus, "My God, my God, why have you forsaken me?" What happened that led to disorder, defeat, loss and disorientation? Where is the God who brought the sunshine? And then, seemingly out of nowhere, comes the sunshine, which brings new life, new gifts and new coherence. Life doesn't return to the familiar, but to our amazement and awe, we are taken to a new place of possibility. That doesn't sound like a storybook, but it does sound like life as I have known it for myself and those I love.

ANATOMY OF ALL PARTS OF THE SOUL

John Calvin had it right—the Psalms are an anatomy of all parts of the soul. Life is like that—seasons of orientation, disorientation and new orientation. Spirituality is like that—seasons of orientation, disorientation and new orientation, all of which call forth faith in various forms. Some seasons call for simplicity of faith, and my prayers are filled with gratitude that God is good and life is coherent; for the moment, at least, God seems present and engaged. But like the earth itself, our lives are in motion, and at some point faith calls for the "dangerous speech" of raw, honest, gritty complaint that life is hard, that God seems distant and disengaged. And sometimes our prayers take on another form of faith with the audacity of gratitude, celebration and joy that God has given life new beauty, glory and hope.

All of the orientations are forms of holy speech in dialogue with God. All of them are forms of prayer. All of them are forms of faith. In the increasingly common dismissal of Scripture in our culture, this point is rarely noticed: the Scriptures in all their strange stories, obtuse texts and challenging words still tell us the truth that life is not easy, and they give us trajectories toward which our lives can become oriented. These poems in all of their varied forms broadcast truth; they are holy dialogue in response to God in which faithful people cry out in praise, lament or celebration and expect God to listen and respond. In 150 different numbered psalms, you find resonant listening. Together and alone, corporately and individually, God invites us to bring all parts of our lives to the table. What seem to be random, disconnected, erratic movements from orientation to disorientation and new orientation, are, in fact, infused with Spirit—not in a formulaic order, but in what can often feel like the chaotic and random flow of a river that has overrun its banks.

The spirituality of the Psalms is life lived with eyes to see and ears to hear, but here's the tricky part: we don't live in a gated spiritual place where life is safe, clearly oriented, comfortable and coherent. Flannery O'Connor once said, "Our age . . . does not have a very sharp eye for the almost imperceptible intrusions of grace."[3] Perhaps it is because they come in many forms; we have learned to look for something "spiritual" or to expect something "mystical" or to listen for something "religious" when instead they come as the unfolding events of our days and nights. But the spirituality of the psalms is ferocious in the face of life's fury. It is poetry for people who can no longer accept the banal, predictable or simplistic because life has never marched in place with easy answers.

The siren that sounds from the Psalms is that God is at work in all of the experiences of life. Someone is present even in the seasons where presence feels more like absence and where coherence is elusive. The people who understand that most are often the elderly, who can see the long horizon of life. When adults return to their childhood home after many years away, the response is often, "It's smaller than I remember it," which means, of course, they saw it in the scale of their childish eyes. The elderly who come to peace with their story come to peace with all of it. They don't embrace it all as equally good or impose a false serenity on chaos or anesthesia on pain. They don't live in fairy-tale memories of their pain. Instead, they practice the spirituality of the psalms in its trilingual speech of orientation, disorientation and reorientation. This is the language of the anatomy of faith: God is present in all of life.

LEARNING TO LISTEN IN AN ORAL CULTURE

I recently sat in on a lecture titled "Orality, Memory and Following Jesus." The professor giving the lecture talked about what he called the psychodynamics of an oral culture. He wasn't talking only about the oral culture of Israel and Jesus' time but about oral culture as a whole. Before there was printing, cultures depended on speech, recitation and listening as the primary form of communication. Even when Scripture was available in written form, the biblical cultures were considered oral cultures. Certain characteristics tend to be evident in oral culture.

1. The reading of texts is repeated. You hear it not once but often. Texts functioned, I think, the way music does for us. We listen repeatedly to songs; if there are lyrics we might sing along aloud or in our heads. We don't listen to them

only once but come to know the song well through repetition. There is the echo of the resonant sounds of presence and voice in surprising places in our universe. The psalms were the repeated texts of worship for Israel and Jesus and still are for many of us. In the rhythm and repetition of liturgy, many congregants hear texts often enough to be comforted or puzzled but at least to be engaged by them.

2. The stories are conserved. Since stories are passed on orally, tradition is repeated as cultural lore. My grandchildren will not let me tell a creative ending to *Green Eggs and Ham* or *The Cat in the Hat*. In an oral culture, stories are known because you heard them told the same way before.

3. The stories are very close to the human world. In all oral cultures, the stories that are remembered are stories of human crisis or celebration or even the commonplace of daily things; they are memorable because they are heard in the context of real life. Imaginative stories and fairy tales are memorable too, but oral cultures tend to repeat stories familiar to the life of the listeners. Perhaps that is why we are raised on comedy, tragedy and fairy tale: art mimics life.

4. Listening is participatory and empathetic—you listen actively. Storytelling and story listening are not spectator sports; listening asks something from you. Different than the physical function of hearing, listening requires attention. In his fiction, Wendell Berry uses the river as a metaphor and physical reality of the presence of mystery. One character reflects back on his family and says, "There had been a time before they came, and a time before that. And always, from a time before anybody knew of time, the river had been there. . . . And I saw how all-of-a-piece it was, how never-

ending—always coming, always there, always going."[4] To say
we learn to become aware of the mystery of presence requires an active and also forgetful kind of listening. We will
need "ears to hear" more than the sounds of humankind
rushing around us but also that which is "never-ending,
always coming, always there, always going."[5]

The poetry of the Psalms was repeated most often in worship
and liturgy as a type of performance. Scholars believe it was not
read in monotone but *enacted* with physicality, gestures and
active reading skills, so as to engage.

The ways Scripture is read aloud in public settings can help
us listen to it. I once had the luxury of spending eight days on a
silent retreat. Each morning I had about ten minutes with a
spiritual director who checked in with me and gave me guidance
for the day ahead. And each morning I had the remarkable experience of listening to him read text to me. "Today," he would
say, "I want you to spend time listening to this story, or question,
or words," and then he would read a biblical text to me. I still
hear the tone of his quiet reading of text in his office. The experience is memorable to me still. He read Scripture; I listened. A
resonance formed in the sound of text being heard out loud. But
I was hungry for meaning in those moments, alert for guidance,
poised for insight. I listened more intently than I usually do. I
wonder if we would hear the voice of God more clearly if
Scripture was read today as it was in an oral culture.

To pray or sing or hear the Psalms read is an intentional way
of saying, "Take all of me, body, mind, spirit and soul." To
practice the faith of the Psalms is to listen when everything says
no one is here, there's no point for your faith or your prayers.
N. T. Wright has said the Psalms call us to live at the intersection

of sacred space, human space and matter,[6] a collision of here, now and all of life. This is faith at its simplest: we listen for God's present voice in sacred space, human space and matter.

The spirituality of the Psalms is an insistent call to listen for the Story in the unfolding of our actual life stories. They seem to say, "Take ownership of your life—all the parts of it. Practice your faith in the ordinary as well as the unexpected extraordinary." Howard Thurman, a great teacher, wrote, "To Jesus, God breathed through all that is."[7] For Thurman, Jesus is the evidence that God is. This notion of the "givenness of God" was a subtext for much of his teaching on human liberation. It is what I mean by the voice of God. If we decide that God's voice was silenced, then we have only to listen to each other. If we decide that God's voice no longer has anything to say, then, again, we are alone in the universe and will listen only to each other, though we don't often do it well. But, I am drawn to the possibility of a voice that can be heard through whispers, songs, wise people, animated reading of Scripture and attentiveness in my own spirit. I am drawn because I believe in the givenness of God. God is here and God is not silent. Jesus voices the word of God in his teachings and in his life. In our distracted culture, Jesus' voice and Jesus' way offer a steadiness and firmness. When we choose to listen and engage we are able to taste, assimilate and eventually to metabolize deep wisdom into every area of our lives.

I don't know who said the following line, but they were on to something: "God often shows up disguised as your life." The spiritual practice necessary is discernment. To discern is to listen deeply . . . but to what? To which voices? Some of you may already have what you would describe as a call from God to a vocation. The Latin word *vocare* is a word that means call, intention and purpose. Some few among us have felt the electricity of God's voice that sparks within, an audible voice or blinding light from beyond. But it doesn't come that way to most of us. More often it seems to come with the timbre of human voices, including our own. Most often it comes as we wonder, ask our questions, seek wisdom and follow our own "hunches." Barbara Brown Taylor says, "The effort to untangle the human words from the divine seems not only futile to me but also unnecessary since *God works with what is. God uses whatever is usable in a life, both to speak and to act,* and those who insist on fireworks in the sky may miss the electricity that sparks the human heart."[8]

WHY I PERSIST

Jesus' most quoted text was the Psalms. Its seemingly contra-dictory texts offer coherence at one time, negativity in the next and surprise yet again—like my life, if not my day, which moves from heights to depths in the space of an email, call or text. There is even authenticity in the rambling arrangement of the psalms. You don't find a section called "orientation," followed by section 2, "disorientation," concluding with section 3, "new orientation." More like my life they seem random, disconnected and scattered. Their arrangement somehow echoes the way life propels us through the entire gamut of emotions. You know I'm telling the truth. The last twenty-four or forty-eight hours, the last seven days and the last year have assaulted you with unex-pected surprise, goodness, glory or pain, and you did not know which would come next. Faith offers a way to prepare for this unrelenting uncertainty. Jewish scholar Abraham Heschel said, "Faith is not an insurance but a constant effort, a constant lis-tening to the eternal voice."[9]

God is not easy. Life is not easy. Today I heard the news that six climbers on Mt. Rainier are dead. Their bodies may never be found. Yesterday a US warrior from Afghanistan was released from five years in a prison. Today he is vilified by some as a deserter. I won't lie to you. Faith is hard. It's a battle at times, a war of spirit and body to listen long enough, deeply enough and perceptively enough to taste wholeness even for a fleeting moment. I am sorry for some of the sermons I preached that promised too much. I am sorry if I ever made it sound easy. I wasn't telling the whole truth. The Psalms will not let me off the hook. Sometimes life is good; sometimes life is devastating, sometimes there is unexpected redemption. But there is no formula except, listen! "He who has ears to hear, let him hear."

One of the great questions I have been asked this past year was, "Why do you persist?" When life's storms assault you and everything in you insists on resisting anything of faith, why do you persist? As the calendar pages turn rapidly and aging takes its toll, why do you persist? After you've experienced the battle-ground of faith and the warfare of spirituality, why do you persist? Anyone who's lived in honesty with their faith for very long has stories to tell of an impulse to turn away or simply turn off the chosen path.

I'm not trained in apologetics, which gives arguments for or an explanation about why people believe. So, I'll come to the question from a deeply personal place because it is a necessary part of the story of any person of faith. I will tell you why I am a Christian or, better, why I am *still* a follower of Jesus, why I persist. You might think, *He's a professional Christian; he has to persist*, or, *He's a Christian because he's a pastor—or has been.* But it may be more accurate to say the opposite; despite the fact that I'm a pastor, I'm still a Christian. Being a pastor has exposed me to the darkness of the human condition, including my own. I have sat in my offices over the years and heard it all, or so it seems sometimes: deep betrayal, inexplicable harm, agonizing and painful disruption, surprising failures.

Ed was one of my first and best teachers of life. He was an alcoholic who lost his first family to his disease and then nearly lost his second family as well. As a young seminary student and pastor, I sat in his tiny apartment with Betty, his second wife, as she cowered in the corner of the room, afraid of what might come next. Ed sat with me and between us was Jim Beam—a full quart of 140-proof Kentucky whiskey. Ed was on a binge and, now, in tears and rage, spat out these words to me: "Just tell me not to drink it, Keith, and I'll stop. Tell me not to drink it right now and I won't." He was in a crisis in the grips of an illness he could not heal on his own. I knew better but I said the words anyway—"Ed, don't drink." And with a searing agony of soul, he cried out in a wailing voice, "Tell me how, please tell me how." He turned his face from me and emptied the bottle as we watched in grief and pain.

A call came from a neighbor who lived down the street. Her husband was in a rage. I ran to the house and heard the shouts and breaking of glass and furniture. The door was open and her husband had a strange, contorted look on his face when I knocked, announced my presence and walked in. I called his name and said, "Stop. Can't you see how much you're scaring your wife and the kids?" He looked at me, a look I have never forgotten; it was somewhere between hatred and disgust. "What would you know about it, pastor?" he spat. With venom he shouted, "You have the perfect life, don't you? Everything works for you. Well, it doesn't work for the rest of us in this f___ing world."

Trauma, abuse, abandonment, betrayal, violence, lust, rage, lies, denial, grief, sickness and fear, and that's on the beginning of the list. But in the end, those stories are the first reason I persist. I have seen the darkness, pain, brokenness and sadness of the human condition, and often enough in myself, and still believe passionately in Jesus Christ because my faith tells the truth about who we are. The contradictions of our lives—of my life—are not a surprise anymore. Over the Rhine songwriter Linford Detweiler crafted the song "What I'll Remember Most" with the memorable line, "You were 80% angel, 10% demon, the rest was hard to explain."[10]

Biblical faith is honest. We are not mildly neurotic or misguided or eccentric; we are fallen, sinful persons. We rebel against the very best that God has for us. We are incapable of achieving the good that we would, says Paul. And you know this, as do I, not only in abstraction but in your own story. There are times when you, like Ed, like David, like me, cannot get it right, no matter how hard you try. But I persist because biblical spirituality tells us the truth. In the presence of God, the Psalms speak that truth right into the face of evil.

Another reason I persist is that I know some people who love Jesus. Anne Lamott wrote an essay about her son titled "Why I Make Sam Go to Church." In it she writes, "The main reason is that I want to give him what I found in the world, which is to say a path and a little light to see by. Most of the people I know who have what I want—which is to say, purpose, heart, balance, gratitude, joy—are people with a deep sense of spirituality. They are people in community, who pray, or practice their faith."[11] Similarly, I persist because I know Ben and Cherie, Lisa and Andy and something called Awake Church and the Aurora Commons in Seattle. Their website is to the point:

The Aurora Commons, located at 8914 Aurora Avenue, is a neighborhood place for hospitality and relationship; a space for holistic renewal through various activities; a bridge to resources (i.e., housing, mental health, addiction, etc.); and a hub for churches, businesses, and neighborhood groups to join together to care to [sic] our neighborhood. The Commons was started by the Awake community in the spring of 2011 after years of working and living with our neighbors who struggle with addiction, house-lessness, mental illness, and sexual exploitation. Together these four are pastors, counselors, community activists and leaders. They created the church and the ministry because they follow Jesus.[12]

I watch them and see them live for the sake of others in a harsh environment. They persist, and that's enough for me.

I persist because I am faced with a claim from Jesus, a claim for a truth that is embodied in him. "I am the way, the truth and the life," he said. Everything in this culture wants me to reject what he said, to put it into a category of opinion and to question its truthfulness. Or to say, "Well, that's fine for you; you're a white, educated, middle-class American. You've spent most of your life in the Midwest. It's not like that everywhere." But the point isn't how well Christianity stacks up against other philosophies or religions; the question is, does Jesus live? If he's alive, then we have no choice—the truth chooses us. God did not send Jesus to give us ideas but to embody the very presence of the living God. In Hebrews, the writer says that Jesus is the living expression of the invisible God. If you want a glimpse at God, the writer says, look at Jesus, there's your portrait of God. The truth claim of Christian faith is that Jesus is who he said he was.

I persist because of the doctrine of redemption. It is another truth claim, Paul said, that scandalizes Jew and Gentile alike. The doctrine of redemption is the claim that Jesus came into the world to redeem us—to serve as a sacrifice of atonement for all of humankind. Christianity would have been an easier sell if he had not made that claim; it could have blended in more easily with the rest of the gods and religions of Paul's day. But he did make the claim. And it was too crazy a claim for Peter or the others to have made it up. If they had invented Christian faith, they could have done it more rationally and made it less scandalous than to claim that Jesus is *the* way. Redemption is foolish. God steps into the created order—into your life and into mine— to love us and to bring us to someplace like home. There is sufficient data to argue for the doctrine of sin, the fall and judgment. I know the list. You have your own list of things that we have done and left undone. Redemption is defiance against the belief that the story ends with human failure, cruelty, violence, betrayal and harm. Redemption is a fierce faith that the world is not finally defined by all that is evil but by the inherent goodness of the creator and redeemer who is alive and still has something to say. I hear the voice of redemption and grace often in the words of the woman I met in the first week of my freshman year in college. A lifetime later she reminds me daily that Jesus is present in her grace, forgiveness, love and delight in me.

And, finally, I persist because of music. It is one of the most profound expressions of human creativity, pointing to something beyond. I remember the evening I sat in Orchestra Hall in Chicago to listen to Gustav Mahler's *Resurrection*, which was new to me at the time. I had heard other Mahler pieces, but that night I was captured by some of the most stunning music I had ever heard in my life. Mahler was not a Christian. He couldn't make the same jump of faith and reason that I have made. But he reflected something in his music that caused my heart to beat wildly and my breath to almost stop. I remember the afternoon I was invited to join some other adult students on a drive out of Boston to something they called "the north shore." I was glad to get out of town for a while and to see something other than reading and papers. As we drove up the coast of the Atlantic, out of Boston, a solo voice played on a CD and I was brought to tears by the beauty of the lyrical soprano voice. Her name is Kiri te Kanawa, a Maori opera singer from New Zealand. I couldn't hear the words of her songs at first, but it didn't matter—the music called something from me that I couldn't name.

Spirituality is hard work because life is often hard work. Anyone who says otherwise reduces life to something less than the pilgrimage it is. Perhaps that's why I remember Abraham Heschel's last interview with NBC journalist Carl Stern when he said, "And above all, remember that the meaning of life is to live life as if it were a work of art."

PRACTICE LISTENING: THE PRAYER OF EXAMEN

Paying attention to all of our story isn't easy. But there are practices that some have found consistently helpful. The prayer of examen is an exercise birthed in the work of Ignatius of Loyola in the sixteenth century. It is a daily practice of guiding one's memory through four steps.

- *Presence:* Remember the presence of God is with us always. Psalm 46:10 says, "Be still, and know that I am God." In the quietness of this reflective time, let your ears tune in to the voice of God; sense the presence of the living God. "The LORD is near to all who call on him, to all who call on him in truth" (Psalm 145:18).

> + Did you sense the presence of God today? How? Where? When?
>
> + Did you practice active listening in the activities of your day?

- *Gratitude:* "If the only prayer you say in your entire life is 'Thank You' that would suffice."[13] Gratitude is as simple as living a life of thankfulness and as complicated as learning to live with a grateful heart. So much of life contests a spirit of gratitude.

> + Looking back on the past twenty-four hours, what are you most grateful for?
>
> + What makes you feel thankful today?

- *Review:* Review the interactions, responses, feelings, interruptions and intentions of the past twenty-four hours. Pause long enough to observe, rather than interpret, justify or rationalize. "Teach me the way I should go, for to you I lift up my soul. . . . Teach me to do your will, for you are my God. Let your good Spirit lead me on a level path" (Psalm 143:8, 10).

> + When or where in the past twenty-four hours were you cooperating most fully with God's action in your life? When were you resisting?
>
> + What habits and life patterns do you notice from the past day?

- *Response:* This is a time to seek forgiveness or direction, or resolve to make changes in your life. Active listening to presence, gratitude and review fuels the time of response.

◆ Beginning today, how do you want to live your life differently?

◆ What patterns do you want to keep living tomorrow?[14]

seven

HEARTBREAK

Listening to Lament

The unwounded life bears no resemblance to the Rabbi.

BRENNAN MANNING

MY WORKPLACE ON THE SEATTLE waterfront faces a
street called Alaskan Way, a street that didn't exist
when the building was built in 1910. It was then just waterfront,
a seawall with docks, and the railroad. Our building was first
used as a fishery and then became the Skyway Luggage
Company for fifty years or more. Now it's a theological graduate
school, a place where very honest questions are asked and
stories told of the pain, abuse, delight and sorrow of life. Our
students are skeptical of packaged faith, as I hope you are. They
have what my friend Sharon Daloz Parks calls big questions
and worthy dreams. They are bold and courageous in asking
questions for which there are often not clear answers, but they
ask them anyway. They aren't quick to accept traditional and

preformed answers for emerging and new challenges. But they bring an intensity of curiosity and a fierce, persistent willingness to listen that gives me hope.

When we took over the building it had stood vacant for years—a relic of downtown Seattle history. The glory of our building was a thing of the past. What once had been new and bright and full of hope was now a shell. The walls were covered with peeling paint from the glory days. The floors were covered with grit, discolored by years of use and abuse. The former utility was gone. But we took it over and did something remarkable. We brought a vision of redemption back into a failed and now flawed place. A story of some of our lives. We had it together once and lost our way. The worst part of the deterioration of the building was the floors: grimy, black, dinged, flawed, scraped and scarred. We sandblasted them, varnished them and left them as they were—scarred, flawed and beautiful. Full of character and honest stories of what had been. I show people the floors every chance I get because they reflect our mission: to find the redemption in each story; to see beauty not only in finished, varnished, perfected products but also beauty that has come because of the scrapes, dings and scars. Beauty that is actually only present in the imperfections.

The great Canadian songwriter and rock singer Leonard Cohen said it best for me in his song called "Anthem." There's a line that echoes in my soul: "There is a crack, a crack in everything. That's how the light gets in."[1] I was not raised to think like that. In my world, scars were a sign of mistakes, failures or accidents. They were to be avoided in our Scandinavian family. If exposed, they were quickly subdued and forgotten. But the cracks aren't magically sealed and the scars aren't all healed. We are not just some of us reclamation projects; we are all in need of grace because we all bump up against life in the night. Unless we are dishonest with ourselves, we all face the limitations of pain, suffering, scars and failure. Now this Canadian musical legend tells me that light comes through the cracks? Through the scars?

Listening is the heart of Christian spirituality. But to listen in the silence? To listen in the darkness? To listen and hear only the sound of your pain, fear or loneliness? Now it sounds like a contradiction or a jarring juxtaposition of ideas. How does God speak to us in the darkness? What does it mean to listen when there is only echoing silence, hollow emptiness? A young slave girl called it "The day life turned into nothing this world could fix."[2]

Surprised by Lament

It was a particularly hot July day in Boston. I was taking classes for professional development in a program that attracted mostly Roman Catholic educators and priests. I am an ordained American Baptist who spends time in Anglican worship these days.

I had been invited to attend the daily worship time on that Wednesday in July. To Gasson Hall I went and joined a group of about seventy people from around the world: the Philippines, El Salvador, Northern Ireland, North America, Australia and England. In the opening words I was invited to worship in a way I had never experienced in any other setting. I was asked to join sisters and brothers of faith to cry out to God in the language of lament. To complain to God about the condition of the world. To decry the violence and shameful oppression under which some in that very room lived. To complain that the universe was not as it should be but instead broken, askew, distorted. To incriminate God for silence, inaction and distance. I held back and remained detached from the prayers of lament because I did not know the language of lament. It was not part of the conservative theology or spiritual practices of my past. But though I had no experience with the language, I knew the experience well. I had lived long enough to know the cry of lament may be more the rule than the exception. What some call *shalom* shattered is not just a rare event; it is the common story of our humanity.

The language of lament is faithful speech addressed authentically to the listening God. It is perhaps the most unexpected source of formation in biblical spirituality. The language includes words of pain, horror, loss, grief, unmitigated suffering and inexplicable agony over the suffering and violence that occurs in the world; it is most dramatic, however, because it complains that God allows such suffering and violence to occur. It incriminates God in our suffering: God knows that we are in pain, and God chooses silence.

The spirituality of lament is not a place most expect to hear the thunder of God's voice. It is a spirituality of "the terribleness of God," as a friend once said. Why does God allow such pain? Why doesn't God intervene to stop the slaughter of innocents in the Congo or Afghanistan or Angola? The poets know the language of lament and speak of human suffering as only they can. The words of Aeschylus were spoken by Robert Kennedy at the death of Martin Luther King Jr., only to be etched into his own gravestone five years later. The inscription echoes the words of any soul who has known grief.

> Even in our sleep, pain which cannot forget falls drop
>   by drop
> upon the heart until, in our own despair, against our will,
> comes wisdom through the awful grace of God.[3]

Like the words of Aeschylus, Psalm 80:4-6 is a cry of unmitigated agony. The writer isn't drafting an intellectual discussion of pain; this writer, one has said, "has been made to eat and drink sorrow."[4]

O LORD God of hosts,
how long will you be angry with your people's prayers?
You have fed them with the bread of tears,
and given them tears to drink in full measure.
You make us the scorn of our neighbors;
our enemies laugh among themselves.

That's the spirituality of lament. "Pain . . . falls drop by drop . . . until . . . comes wisdom through the awful grace of God." Listening doesn't promise to be a satisfying experience. Sometimes we listen in utter darkness. Sometimes we listen in the pain of unimaginable grief. Sometimes the only honest act of faith is to sit in the face of the worst that life can do to us. Why then listen at all?

Dan Allender wrote once that "Christians seldom sing in the minor key. We fear the somber; we seem to hold sorrow in low-esteem. We seem predisposed to fear lament as a quick slide into doubt and despair; failing to see that doubt and despair are the dark soil that is necessary to grow confidence and joy."[5] Instead we seem ready to embrace the words in *Harry Potter and the Prisoner of Azkaban*, "Happiness can be found even in the darkest of times if one only remembers to turn on the light."[6] There's a sense of optimism in that sentiment, but lament is a ferocious act of faith in the moments when one cannot even find the light.

Pain, sorrow, suffering, sadness and failure all separate us from one another. They move us into a place of isolation. Lament brings us together in a community of tears. In my early years in pastoral ministry I was assigned each week a list of "shut-ins" to go and visit. Shut-ins were shut out of the life of community in the church. Unable to participate in worship, fellowship or practices of community, they were marginalized by their pain unless the church or community remembered them and cared for them in their isolation. Something happens when pain is shouted to God in lament by a community of tears.

God Is on Our Side

On Sunday, September 15, 1963, as Sunday school was in session, a white supremacist terrorist bombed the 16th Street Baptist Church in Birmingham, Alabama. Four girls, three age fourteen and one eleven, were murdered by the blast. The scene depicting this incident is horrific and powerful in the movie *Selma*. In the aftermath of the disaster, doors open and four caskets are carried out bearing the bodies of the four girls murdered in church. On my desk is a medallion I purchased as I walked within the walls of that place of disaster and violence. It shows the clock at the exact moment the explosion hit and froze the moment in time. What is striking to me is that three of those four girls were exactly my age when they were brutally taken by the violence of racism. The medallion clock is stopped at precisely 10:21 when the bomb exploded and tore out the walls where these children were engaged in learning of Jesus. In point of fact they were in an assembly preparing for the sermon that day, "The Love That Forgives." It is the moment of their exit from the church on the way to the cemetery when an unidentified voice from the crowd began to do what spiritual people always end up doing—she began to sing and her words spoke of impossible faith in a moment of inexplicable loss. "God is on our side," came the first halting words. "God is on our side," she sang and soon others joined in those words, which I doubt anyone actually felt in that moment. "God is on our side . . . we shall overcome." She did something so extraordinarily impossible that it could only be done by someone who still believed. She connected their story to gospel and subverted the awful reality of their grief. She declared what Christians have always believed: God is not finished, even when it seems to be the end. There is a crack, a crack in everything. That's how the light gets in.

So why do we bring lament to God at all? Why bother? Will there be an answer? Will there be relief? Is there resolution? I listened to a writer recently tell his story. He was thirteen when they learned the news that his brother was dying. The young pastor of their church came to the hospital and spoke words that would define his life for many years: "If you will pray and if your heart is pure, your brother will be healed." Just days later, his brother died. Something is destroyed in us in such a moment, do we see that? Something is taken from us in an act of violence when we are given a facile formula in such a moment. There is no formula for some of the harshest moments of our lives. Sometimes we must simply sit in the darkness. The answer to lament in the Psalms must wait for Jesus' words in Matthew's Gospel, "Blessed are those who mourn."

The honest and earthy spirituality of the psalms of lament are a necessary balance to the easy spirituality of songs of victory that ignore the adversity and suffering of God's people around the world. It was uncanny in that July noontime worship service because the longer we prayed the closer I felt to my Catholic friends, even though I am very different from them in background, practices and community. We didn't end the service with joyful songs of triumph. We ended the service with quiet songs of faith. It wasn't about answers, victories or solutions. It was about faith, honest faith, earthy faith, real faith. What do you do with the deepest, most painful cries of your breaking heart? What my faith community tended to deny or sublimate these sisters and brothers from El Salvador and Northern Island named boldly out loud. The faith community says that we are to bring that breaking heart to speech in lament to our God.

ON THE ANVIL OF SUFFERING: JOB'S STORY OF LAMENT

"There was once a man in the land of Uz whose name was Job. That man was blameless and upright, one who feared God and turned away from evil" (Job 1:1). Job was not just successful, he was sincere in his faith, honest in his morality, faithful in his integrity. And then it all came undone. Right at the moment when he had achieved every goal he could possibly have in his purpose-driven life, it all came unglued. In a fierce assault from the adversary, he was systematically stripped of everything he possessed until Job found himself about as desolate a human being as ever existed. And that's the picture the writer wants to present: Job was on the anvil, in the heat, being pounded by life and forged into something that didn't look anything at all like his old life.

Faith understands that suffering and pain are woven into the fabric of life. Job's saga shows us that they are part of the human story. In chapter 10, Job raises his voice in complaint to the Creator. "I loathe my life; I will give free utterance to my complaint: I will speak in the bitterness of my soul. I will say to God, Do not condemn me; let me know why you contend against me. Does it seem good to you to oppress, to despise the work of your hands and favor the schemes of the wicked?" (Job 10:1-3). Similarly, Alan Jones says, "I look at the world, I look at my country, I look at myself. There rises up in me a voice that says, Surely God could do better than this! My disappointment easily slips into anger and resentment. Somewhere deep inside me there comes a bitter cry, Life isn't meant to be like this! It isn't meant to be full of pain and tragedy. I beg to return my ticket."[7]

Listening stops when grieving begins. Adrenaline is pumped into the body and chemical reactions take place that create tears, fear, pain, panic and deep sadness. We all grieve in our own way. Some are silent while others wail in loud agony. Some are stoic and appear strong while others are emotionally ravaged and appear weak. When the news of tragic loss and death is given there is one universal word of response: it is the word of denial, "No!" "It cannot be true, no, that's not possible." Our bodies and minds unite to protect against the unthinkable—someone we love is dead. And then the universal stages of grief identified so long ago by Elisabeth Kübler-Ross take over:

- Denial is the defense against the unthinkable. We block the news and try to block the truth.

- Anger is our response to pain—directed at almost everyone and anything.

- Bargaining is an attempt to make a deal with our overwhelmed feelings of helplessness.

- Depression is sadness, regret, worry and fear: it may last a short time or be spread over many days or weeks, but ultimately it prepares us for the final stage of acceptance.

- Acceptance is when a sense of equilibrium returns, though the pain, sadness and grief may accompany us always.

Spirituality does not stop when we grieve. Biblical spirituality is not a spirituality of the denial of loss, pain, grief and death; it is a spirituality that calls us to continued attention even in the midst of our pain.

Is it okay to bring our cries of lament to God? Does your theology allow you to complain to God? As you seek to integrate theology and practice, worldview and life, what do you do when the anvil experience is yours or comes to those about whom you care? If your faith is nurtured by reading the book of Psalms or the book of Job, you know that we have an entire body of literature from God that does exactly that: a large proportion of Psalms are the complaints of people—as individuals and as a nation—raising their laments of pain and suffering to a God whom they aren't always sure cares to listen to their cries. Psalms of lament come from individuals in personal pain and suffering; they come from the nation as they plead their case in the midst of war, crisis and carnage.

There is a biblical language that shapes us as the people of God. There is a grammar of faith, a syntax and certainly a vocabulary that is uniquely ours, and we give up this language at great risk to the faithfulness of our spirituality. We have traded in this language of lament for something far less: the language of grief management or psychology. When we trade biblical vocabulary for the vocabulary of the culture, we are increasingly subject to losing our ability to hear this language. Lament is biblical language. It is *our* language—the grammar of our faith, the vocabulary of our native tongue. Jesus spoke it from the cross, quoting the lament of Psalm 22; David sang it often, and the Jews spoke it, sang it and lived it as a natural and necessary part of the practice of their spirituality. Lament is the honest speech of the people of God faithfully addressed to the listening

God. Some scholars tell us that over 40 percent of the psalms are ones in which people of faith bring their laments, their complaints to God. The sheer volume and intensity of lament throughout Old Testament writings call us to reclaim this silenced language of our native tongue.

Lament isn't just noticing in some dispassionate way that life is hard; it leads us into testimony that cries out in vivid speech how life is almost unbearable. Lament is language where everything is not polite and civil. Through hyperbole, vivid imagery and emotion, psalms of lament move us "from life well-ordered into an arena of terror, raggedness, and hurt. In some sense this speech is a visceral release of the realities and imagination that have been censored, denied, or held in check by the dominant claims of society."[8] They cause us to think unthinkable thoughts and utter unutterable words. Bruggemann has called it "the resilience of the darkness" in spite of religious attempts to manage, control and eliminate it.[9] I sat with the director of a local theater in Seattle who was at our faculty retreat to talk about how a director's work might compare to the work of teachers. One line captured my imagination more than the rest. He said, "A lighting designer is also a shadows designer." We live in both light and shadows. With light comes shadows—it's a simple fact of science.

So, I ask, is lament bold faith or a failure of faith? For ancient Israel, it was decidedly an act of faith, boldly brought to the One whom they believed was also listening. Honest faith, bold faith insists that

- we experience the world as it really is and life as it comes to us, all of it;

- pain, suffering, trauma, disorder and horror are legitimate complaints to bring to God;

- if we are honest, we have no choice but to cry out in lament in such moments; and

- everything in the human experience must be brought in words to God. Something happens when we say the words out loud, when God listens.

I live in a part of the world that isn't sure the Christian community is honest enough to be of any use to them. Some of them look at the church and wonder if our questions really matter to anyone outside of the gated community of the church. Some of them wonder if we know how to be authentic at all or if prepackaged answers are all we have. Some of them live not knowing more than the false security of easy answers. And some find the church to be a place of abuse, toxicity, harm and pain; lament, it seems, has been their only language of faith.

One of our staff is an alumnus who, with his wife, lived for the birth of their son. A first child. A lifelong hope and longing. All that new life—your life embodied in your child—would bring. The day before the delivery due date Christine knew something was wrong. She couldn't feel any movement from her son. Just hours before the greatest moment of their life they learned the worst possible truth—Jackson was dead in the womb. And still she had to deliver little Jackson. She had to feel the pain without the reward of her child alive in her arms. Together they held the lifeless body of the son they would never know. The funeral a few days later was unlike anything in my life. Andrew and Christine carried in the tiny coffin and never let go. They grieved aloud and took us all into their grief with them. They mourned and wailed and cried out to little Jackson, to one another, to God. One of their pastors is Andy Carlson, another alumnus, a pastor, and a carpenter-artist. He stood and said, "I am undone. As a church we are undone. If you came for something neat and packaged you will not find it here today. If you came for answers, you might leave without finding them. If you thought we could help you with your questions, you might be wrong." He then paused for a long time. And then some minutes later he said, fighting back his tears, "Still, still I believe in resurrection. I still believe."

In the face of the worst that life can bring, in the honesty of raw human suffering, there is a crack, a crack in everything. That's how the light gets in. Sometimes you just have to sit in your life and hurt.

Lament *is* an act of faith. That's what we all discovered. We brought our complaints to the right listener. We carried our laments to the one who invites us to bring *all* our burdens to him, to cast *all* our cares on him. We lifted our voices to the God who knows and agonizes over human suffering as much as we do. We brought our prayers—all of them—to God. And we brought our honest prayers together as a community of God's people. Sometimes it is just too difficult to be Christian alone. Christian faith was never intended to be something you do all by yourself. For the trusting community, the use of lament is *an act of bold faith* because it insists that the world must be experienced honestly, that we must receive it as it really is. Walter Brueggemann says in lament there is nothing out of bounds, nothing precluded or inappropriate. Lament insists that everything must be brought to speech and addressed to God, who is the final reference for all of life.[10]

When Job brought his suffering to God, God seemed to be indifferent to his pain, but Job was in no position to understand ultimate answers, even if they had been given to him. Such answers belong to the realm of the infinite, and he was a finite creature. This was one of the errors intellectualizing caused Job to make. He had forgotten who he was and the *limits* to his being. The kind of explanations Job had been demanding of God were utterly beyond him. Do you want to know why there is undeserved suffering in the world? Why there is injustice? Why there is heartache? "Here's my answer," says God. "Where were you when I laid the foundation of the world? Tell me. . . . Have you commanded the morning since your days began?" In fact, God never does give Job an answer. Instead he asks him sixty-four questions in a row. For four chapters the voice of God talks about ostriches, wild asses and hippopotami. God's answer is: "Can you create an ostrich?"

The ancient rabbis wrestled with the same questions we have, and they came up with the same answer: we don't know. There are limits to what we can comprehend. God paraded the whole drama of creation before Job and then refocused his attention: God turned him around with an astonishing observation. God is found in the midst of the suffering. Better than answers, says the book of Job, is the presence of God in the whirlwind.

Psalm 23, one most people seem to love, is stark and shattering in its honesty: "Even though I walk through the darkest valley, I fear no evil" (v. 4). The geography in that sentence is crucial. I do not walk *around* the darkest valley. I do not walk *away* from the darkest valley. I am not catapulted *over* the darkest valley as a kind of reward for my faith. I walk *through* the darkest valley; I walk *into* the times of darkness and pain. I walk *by way of* the darkest valley. In Jesus' Sermon on the Mount he tells us we are blessed, made happy. What I have learned recently is that Jesus' word choice for "blessed" means on the right road. It is pathway language—language that takes us through, into, by way of.

I don't know why you persist, if indeed you do. We've all lived long enough to know the cracks in ourselves if we've been listening. We know there are holes, flaws, and stories of abuse and trauma and failure—done to us and by us. There's a crack, a crack in everything, that's how the light gets in. But I know that listening in the darkness is an act of faith every bit as much as listening in the light. Listening and demanding a hearing with God is bold, honest faith in inexplicable pain. North Americans deny pain, it seems. We anesthetize it, shuttle it away from our eyes and silence the sound of it. But we cannot escape it.

But what if Leonard Cohen got it right, after all? He found no answer, but like the church in Birmingham, he had music. "There's a crack, a crack in everything, that's how the light gets in." It's not just good poetry, it's not just good theology. It's the story I have lived with trusted friends. It's what still keeps me on the journey.

PRACTICE LISTENING: A BRIEF SERVICE OF LAMENT

My worship experience never included lament until that day in July. I learned that day that lament almost seems to demand a community at worship. I can grieve alone, I believe, but lament is communal, something we do together. I don't know who wrote the words I include below. In my files was the rough outline for a service of lament. The anonymity of those who crafted this service joins us together around this most common human need: to give voice to our lament and cry out to God, asking God to listen.

> **Unison prayer:** We are a wounded people. We are a suffering people. We are a people who long for healing, relief and peace in the midst of

lives that feel torn and ravaged. We know that in your mystery there is healing and presence through our wounds. But we have gathered as a people undone seeking to name the hurts in our lives, the pain in our souls, the questions that have no answers. In bold faith, we come today to say that we bring our complaints to you, our God.

Silent prayer: We individually ask the Holy Spirit to be present to us as we pray in silence.

READING: PSALM 13

The complaints of the people

Worship leader: Together we make known our cries of lament. We cry out to you, God,

- for the needs of children and elderly
- for stress, distress and anxiety (Psalm 42)
- for the needs of the poor (Psalm 44)
- for the needs of the politically oppressed (Psalm 60)
- for the needs of war-ravaged nations (Psalm 43)
- for the needs of the sick, suffering and dying (Psalm 38)
- for prayers that seem to be met without answers
- for pain that seems to never to heal
- for grief that is like a wound that never heals

Individual prayers of lament are invited. Each person will bring their cry of lament to God. At the end of each lament they will say, "Let us bring our laments to the Lord." The response of the congregation is, "Lord, hear our prayers."

READING: PSALM 98

Let us pray.

Help us, O Lord, to see in our woundedness an invitation to new life, to let go of the past and to walk into the future.

Help us, O Lord, to believe that the suffering that is part of our lives is a way to break the boundaries of what we thought we could bear, and to open us to a larger sense of what life is all about.

Help us, O Lord, to accept the suffering in our lives as a sacred wound through which a new story, the good news, is breaking through.

Liturgist: God, Creator and Lord, through these prayers of lament, grant us your comfort. When we are afraid, give us courage. When afflicted, give us patience. When dejected, give us hope, and when alone, assure us through the support of your holy people. We ask this through Christ our Lord, amen.

eight

WHAT WE DON'T WANT TO HEAR

The Prophetic Voice

*What a hideout: holiness lies spread and borne
over the surface of time and stuff like color.*

Annie Dillard

THERE ARE PEOPLE WHOSE WORDS speak of God with a clarity that I don't want to hear. As much as I claim to want a clear word from God, I have an instinct to run from people who have that kind of word. I wonder about you too. There have been people who have heard the voice of God with distinctive clarity—prophets who declared a message the people did not want to hear. The job you least wanted to have in the eighth century BC was that of prophet. Their job was to bring a word with such clarity that everyone knew the truth of the words; the problem was most people did not want to hear the message they brought. Yet they were words God needed the

people to hear. Sometimes what we most need to hear is what
we are least open to hear. The title of one of Walter Brueggemann's books provocatively captures the power of prophetic
words: *Words That Linger, Texts That Explode*.[1]

Not Inclined to Listen

The book of Amos offers a startling word of prophetic warning
and critique in the midst of a worship revolution in ancient
Israel. Religious life was vivid and alive as people flocked to the
places of worship. You would think it was a good thing, but it
turns out otherwise. The ears of the people were not inclined to
listen to truth, so Yahweh sent a loud, intrusive voice into their
midst to get their attention. It was the God they did not want
to hear; it was not the God they would have chosen.

Amos spoke his thunderous words in the eighth century BC.
The northern kingdom of Israel had reached its summit of pros-
perity and power, their greatest enemy was defeated, and there
was contentment in the land—but not for all. War-weary, this
postwar generation turned to fascinating things such as wealth,
material luxuries, indulgent excess and worship.

Life in the new empire in Judah was likewise splendid. Af-
fluence was the new normal for part of the population, and worship
was popular across the nation. Economic well-being and religious
fervor walked hand-in-hand. Newfound wealth and political
power seemed a sure sign of divine favor. And then along came
Amos claiming he had heard the voice of God with a message his
fellow citizens did not want to hear. In a loud voice he told them
something was amiss. And once Amos opened his mouth to tell
them what he saw, the people wanted to silence him.

It's one thing to see your success as a sign of God's gracious
goodness; it is another to believe it is deserved even as you cast

a deaf ear to the sounds of the poor. The time period was marked by nationalism, national optimism and national pride. Trade led to exploding wealth for a new and powerful merchant class. There was also judicial corruption, economic oppression and religious fervor fueled by entitlement; they believed their success was somehow deserved and given to them by God. Lavish wealth existed across the street from abject poverty, human slavery and hunger. The courts extorted the poor, and the religious shrines blindly became tools in the service of the state. Into that setting Amos brought a thundering and frightening word of judgment. His answer was "No!" He declared that Israel was "out of plumb," no longer true or within their standards as the people of God and that judgment was inevitable; God would act to make things right again.

THE LARGE WORLD OF THE BIBLE

The word *prophet* means "a voice of God." They were poets whose words intended to draw listeners into the alternative world of God's movement in history. Eugene Peterson said it best:

> As long as we're ignorant of the Scriptures we won't have a clue as to what God is doing. We do need to recover the large world of the Bible. What I see happening is that when people read the Bible, they reduce the world to something which they call Bible study. But the world of the Bible, the world revealed in Scripture, is a much larger world than anything you get in the newspapers or history books. If we're doing Bible study right we ought to get a glimpse of that.[2]

We can get lost in the detail, so I return to the simplicity of biblical spirituality: God is interested not only in what we do *in the sanctuary of worship* but in what we do *everywhere else* as well. That is the insistent echoing voice from Scripture. God's presence is not limited to a place (church) or a process (worship) or a time (Sunday morning or the various times for "church") but is found at all times in all places. God is at work in the world to heal, restore and redeem.

The prophetic claim is that God is unwilling to put up with worship corrupted by violence, injustice and indifference to the poor. Prophetic spirituality is not critical of worship per se, although the words are sharply edged and, well, prophetic. It insists on an integration of all of life and not a separation of worship, faith, spirituality and God apart from the rest of what we do. Prophetic spirituality today might be called organic, holistic or integrative. It rails against compartmentalization of faith into a gated part of our lives. It assesses worship from the perspective of the streets and marketplace instead of the sanctuary. The thunder of the prophets declares that God makes a claim on all of life. Spirituality is grounded, quite literally, in earthiness, in time and place. God's presence is in all things; there is no separation between worship and work, prayer and life.

The prophetic voice is a call to live with integrity in all of life. But much is revealed in the details: Finance and economics matter to God. The legal system and justice matter to God. Banking policies matter to God. Treatment of the poor, the marginalized, the widows and the orphans matter to God. Sexual practices and sexual morality matter to God too, a word that many today are most resistant to hear. If we step back and listen again to the prophets, we hear a word about being whole, integral, having coherence. The simple message of prophetic spirituality is about integrity between the various sectors of our lives. Worship with deep, heartfelt conviction finds integrity in how we handle the other parts of our lives. Justice is a core value to the God whose voice is heard through the prophets like Amos, Isaiah and Hosea. Fidelity to the voice of God in the sanctuary ought to lead to fidelity in every corner of our lives.

Prophetic spirituality is not a separate spirituality as much as a corrective to the limitations of all other spiritualties. Without the prophetic word, we have succumbed to an enculturated worship of experience; we prefer what is new, innovative and current even if there is no deep, historical anchor; we prefer truncated forms of sentiment instead of theological substance. If we do not hear the words of the prophets and let their consciousness penetrate the worship of the church, we silence the voice of God. That is a bold claim, but the history of the church bears it out as the church has succumbed to merely cultural forms of worship at numerous stages of its history. Human slavery was not only defended on biblical grounds but considered faithful to the voice of God. Economic exploitation has been likewise defended as the intention of God without regard to the needs of the very same poor and marginalized ones about whom the prophets were so focused. Exploitation of the earth has been defended as God's will on the basis of the imminent return of Jesus. Racial superiority has been defended as a word from God, as has been sexism, nationalism, ethnic superiority and all forms of economic classism. The God we do not want to hear is one whose voice challenges much of what we claim as our theological entitlement, as did ancient Israel.

Prophetic spirituality is also a bold statement about a God whose voice is not domesticated into merely religious interest. It shows God's concern for the whole of a person's life, including political, social, economic, judicial and moral issues. It is a spirituality that wants us to move from the sanctuary into the marketplace, courthouse, medical center, educational institutions, the arts, banking, investment houses and businesses both small and large. The prophet's words are systemic; that is, they are not directed to an individual but to an entire culture. God's concern is for the whole nation—the people and the culture. God will not let us see the spiritual journey as one in which we fly solo; we are part of a larger story of God's intentions for all people. The prophets speak harsh words that are hard for some of us to hear because they are words of judgment about how we separate our faith from acts of justice, equity and morality in all things.

> When you stretch out your hands,
>   I will hide my eyes from you;
> even though you make many prayers,
>   I will not listen;
> your hands are full of blood.

> Wash yourselves; make yourselves clean;
>   remove the evil of your doings
>   from before my eyes;
> cease to do evil,
>   learn to do good;
> seek justice,
>   rescue the oppressed,
> defend the orphan,
>   plead for the widow. (Isaiah 1:15-17)

AN ALTAR IN THE WORLD

I once taught a course that I called An Altar in the World. The title came from Barbara Brown Taylor's book in which she claims that our life is lived, all of it, in one universe, not in a Gnostic kind of detached spirituality of many worlds. There isn't the kingdom of God in one part of life here and the kingdom of this world over here. There aren't separate realities. God moves in all of the sectors of life that matter to us:

- economics and finance
- politics and power
- the law and justice
- education and thought
- healthcare and bodies
- business and jobs
- sanctuaries and worship
- culture and the arts

The subtext for the prophets is that what we tend to separate into categories of sacred and secular are in fact all sacred. What we tend to isolate as sanctuary and workplace are, in fact, both altars for worship. Prophetic spirituality is jarring because it won't let us keep separate our life in the sanctuary and our life at work.

Every job has a workspace. For some of us it is a desk. In the world of religion, the sacred desk may be a pulpit for proclamation or an altar for Eucharist. It is a holy place of liturgy, Scripture, word and sacrament. For my father, a lithographer, his workspace was often in his car as he traveled to printing houses in and around Chicago to sell the artwork the lithographic plate makers created in his shop with cameras, cutting tables and color wheels. My mother's workspace was our home—a kitchen table, kitchen sink and household—but it was often, ironically, also the family car as she delivered five children to activities, jobs and events. For some it is a surgical table or examination table in a medical facility. For others it is a lectern, white board and classroom. For some it is a tractor, plow, and textbooks to study agronomy, weather and veterinary science. For others it is a desk, conference room and computer linked to the business of securities, government, banking, finance and commerce. The poetry of the prophets proclaims that we all have our own altar in the world because we serve God in all of the ways we serve others. If that creates a shift in your way of seeing your work, then welcome home to the world created by God. God's house, says another poet, is the whole earth. God's work, therefore, is not limited to what a few ordained clergy do but includes what we all do when we are listening, paying attention, serving at our own altar in the world.

Amos, Isaiah, Micah—the whole lot of them—were intense, even shrill, in their insistence that God's imagination includes all of this. Barbara Brown Taylor's imagery is gentler but just as insistent—all of us have an altar in the world.[3] All of us stand or sit at the sacred place of work. All of us offer sacrifice (worship) to God in the dailyness of our jobs. All of us have holy business to conduct in our vocations. All of us love God and neighbor as we take our place at our altar in the world. The prophetic voice subverts our tendency to compartmentalize our life into categories. Category A: the spiritual stuff; category B: the rest of life, that is, the "real" stuff. Subverting our thinking about spirituality restores us to the dominion work of Genesis 1—to the celebration of the earth, creation, our bodies and the daily routines of our work. Prophetic spirituality is a cry for coherence. Bring integrity, the prophets say, to your worship, work and world. What is easily fragmented or isolated—worship and work—belongs in a common spirituality of coherent faith.

From the earliest moments of creation it was made clear that we are workers made to work for the common good in the world. We reflect the image of God as worker, creator, designer, builder, architect and artist. God is known first in creation as a worker. I have played imaginatively with images of worker that might be hinted at in the creation texts: God as an electrician who created light in the world, or an agriculturalist who created trees, anesthesiologist who puts the man to sleep prior to surgery, surgeon who removes the rib, musician who gives the earth's creatures voice, designer who builds systems, ecologist who cares for the environment, politician who hands governance to humankind, physician who heals the man, and seamstress who sews loincloths to cover their shame. The list is fanciful but suggestive of God whose interests include earth, sky, sea, plants, animals and people—ecosystems, human systems, bodily systems and rationality.

What is less fanciful is my running list of vocations in biblical texts: shepherds, fishermen, teachers (rabbis), kings and princes, we might all know, but keep on: farmers, miners, lawyers, judges, physicians, tanners (leather workers), warriors, servants, householders, bankers, priests, scribes, seers (magi), poets, childcare workers, prison guards, chefs, gardeners, builders, morticians, sailors, swineherds, tax collectors, soldiers, government officials, wedding planners, musicians (flute players), day laborers, housekeepers, bakers, millers, vintners, financial wealth managers, landowners, investors, animal husbandry workers, students, janitors, dishwashers, gravediggers, tailors, perfumers, gardeners, police, treasurers, governors, hunters, dancers, stone masons, merchants, nursemaids, midwives, goldsmiths, silversmiths, laundry workers, harpists, trumpeters, innkeepers, magicians, tentmakers, watchmen, blacksmiths, counselors, brick makers, couriers, engravers, bodyguards, hunters, magistrates, philosophers, preachers, weavers and construction workers not to mention bandits, prostitutes, spies and thieves.

When the Cistercian monk Thomas Merton moved to the abbey of Gethsemani in Kentucky in 1945, he declared his concern with "doing ordinary things quietly . . . for the glory of God."[4] My father was a businessman, co-owner of a small business in Chicago. Along with his best friend, another first-generation American son of Swedish immigrants, they came to own the company and care for its fifty employees for forty years. In the last coherent conversation I had with my father as he slipped into Alzheimer's, he cried and said, "My life didn't count for much because I wasn't a preacher or missionary or religious man." I was incredulous and then angry, very angry. "How can you say that?" I asked. "For forty years you were the steward of resources that provided everything for over fifty families—food, homes, clothing, education, transportation, entertainment, health care, music and life!" How could he not see his life as honorable, successful and godly? And then I remembered. All of his life he too was the victim of a view of the world called Gnosticism foisted on us from the first century. It separates the world into two categories: spiritual and material. The Gnostics taught that only that which is spiritual is good. In fact, the body was considered the prison of the soul. It claimed the spirit was held captive, against its will, we could almost say, in the physical, material and human. So the world is split—the important things are spiritual, the rest is unimportant. Spirit matters. Bodies do not. Religion is primary; everything else is secondary. And I saw how this was translated for my father: business is about material things so it doesn't matter. Religion counts; the marketplace doesn't—except to fund churches, charities and religious orders. Prayer is important; work is not. Clergy do the work of God; everyone else does something less.

But I'm Not Ordained

October 1975 it was. Pontiac, Michigan, on the corner of Huron and Mark Street. A Sunday morning that celebrated my ordination to Christian ministry. The church had called me (recognized a vocation for ministry in me), examined me (studied my fitness for ministry), laid hands on me (to symbolize their readiness to claim me as their own) and ordained me (authorized me for the work of word and sacrament, that is, to preach, baptize, serve as liturgist at Eucharist, and all things religious in our congregation). It is a precious memory for me (except for the reversible tweed, brown plaid three-piece suit from JCPenney that I wore). It was a sacred action by the church. Ordination is an ecclesiastical act of consecration when a congregation sets one aside for holy work (Christian ministry). It set me apart from others for something sanctified, holy, spiritual. But ordination only tells part of the story of ministry in the world. All of us go with a sacred task into our jobs. All of us are given an altar in the world.

On another October in a college chapel, several dozen faculty walked to the front of the Great Hall with symbols of their work—a textbook by a historian, poetry by a literature professor, a laser by a physicist, clay by an artist, spreadsheets by an economist, syllabi by a professor, a stethoscope by a nursing professor, sheet music by a musician, and a basketball by a coach. They were placed on the floor of the stage, which became, in that instant, an altar in the world. We laid hands on the symbols of their work, and we prayed for, consecrated, blessed and "ordained" those faculty from all sectors of a liberal arts college for their work in the lives of students. We sent them out as Paul and Timothy, Luke, Silas, Priscilla, Aquila and others had been sent out before: "in the name of Jesus." We got it right that day, though sadly, we didn't do it often.

Your work, no less than your worship, is holy work when it is done listening for the voice of the creative God. There are not holy times and holy places that are more important than ordinary times and workplaces. There is simply different work to be done. Worship is time set apart for *leitourgia*, the work of the people. It is a time for communal focus on God in particular forms of listening to Scripture, prayer and song. It is a time set apart but not more holy or sacred because of the task. Worship is a way for us to know that all of life is sacred. We have been taught to ask the wrong questions. Instead of "Which activity is more holy than another?" the better question is "What can you give in this moment?" Annie Dillard writes, "Spend the afternoon, you can't take it with you."[5] The life of the spirit is lived in the life of the body, not somewhere else. Listening for the voice of God ultimately leads to vocation, a call to serve God at the altar of our lives. The practice of listening is neither narcissistic nor merely individualistic; it moves us from the heart of God to the needs of the neighborhood. In Jesus' life it was the downward journey from a throne room to a stable, a carpenter's workbench, a countryside for public teaching and finally to a cross. For some it leads from a seminary desk to a pulpit or sanctuary, but for all of us it leads to *vocare*, finding our place in God's world.

For all their holy anger at the people for their sin, it is not worship, but the distortion of worship and life, that holds the gaze of the prophets. It is when we are comfortable in the sanctuary and uncaring in the street. It is when we are passionate with the congregation in the singing of hymns but indifferent to the poor in their struggle for food. It is when we are caught up in mystical spirituality in worship but leave God there as we go to work. Amos's message is not hard to understand: God expects integral worship, an authentic connection between the sanctuary and the courtroom, worship center and marketplace, church and society.

Compartmentalization has long been a problem for the church; we disconnect what God intends to be connected, we disembody what God desires to reincarnate. "In the beginning was the Word . . . and the Word became flesh and lived among us" (John 1:1, 14). Some wit has said that the church has done a great job of taking the flesh and making it word again, disembodying that which God wants us to embody. Understanding the concept that God is interested in all of life isn't difficult. For many of us, however, we have to unlearn the division of life into sacred and secular, holy and other. Spending time in worship is one way we understand that all time is sacred.

Our English word "worship" comes from an old Anglo-Saxon word that means "to ascribe worth" or "to honor." The Old Testament word used for worship means "a bowing down," declaring to us that worship is active; it is something you do. In fact, it is something you decide to do. Like listening, worship asks that we pay attention. To worship is to attribute supreme worth to God for who God is and what God does. It is to honor or attribute worth, to validate or highly value. It is to say YES to someone or something. It is to pay attention to the already active presence of God. Sometimes it takes all I have in me to listen in worship. I am distracted and easily sidetracked; and then something rooted in the universe gets hold of me and I know I have heard the voice that draws from me a trembling amen.

Listen to the words of the apostle John. They are the quintessential statement of worship: "You are worthy, our Lord and God, to receive glory and honor and power, for you created all things" (Revelation 4:11). Worship of God may take an individual on a walk in the wind or take a community to liturgy in a sanctuary. Biblical spirituality was formed by a nation that practiced worship in all settings:

- at home around the dinner table in daily prayer

- in the home around a family altar in the observance of sabbath

- in the temple for periodic holy festivals and gatherings

- in sacred places gathering to wait on the Lord in silent anticipation

- in sacred assembly

- in liturgies and annual feasts

- in ordinary time

Amos's cry does not remove us from the world of economic policies, judicial practices, social mores and political realities in the name of Spirit; rather, it takes us *into* the world of economics, politics, justice and society fully aware that all of this *is* spiritual. In worship we are ushered into a world that is more, not less, real than the world of the marketplace. Worship is not an action intended to isolate us from the mundane world of checkbooks, newspapers, diapers and oil changes. Worship helps us understand, however, that all of life is intensely spiritual. That is why Amos can speak with such clarity: "Do not separate what God intends as one." In one of his prayers, Walter Brueggemann says,

Here we are, practitioners of memos: We send e-mail and we receive it, we copy it and forward it and save it and delete it. We write to move the data, and organize the program, and keep people informed—and know and control and manage. We write and receive one-dimensional memos, that are, at best, clear and unambiguous. And then—in breathtaking ways—you summon us to song.[6]

It would be our mistake to decide that worship is unimportant because the prophets brought such stern critique. It is, instead, because the prophets loved worship that they insisted on integrity in worship that would be lived out practically in all things. Theirs was a community of people formed by daily prayer, weekly Sabbath and regular worship. They knew that formation is a slow process that requires patience. Over the years of life, we are formed into a Christlike shape through the work of God's Spirit and of God's people in gathered worship.

SURPRISED BY LISTENING IN CHURCH

My line of sight to the chancel was unblocked. The preacher of the morning was readying herself to proclaim the word. It was quickly clear to us all she had studied the text well. But then I saw something unexpected. Perhaps it was the tilt of her head that gave it away or the inquisitive squint of her eyes, but something told me a shift was happening to her. The look said to me she heard something she had not already discovered in her exegetical study or metabolized in previous readings of the text. I was a witness to a living moment of revelation. As she spoke to us, she was listening to the presence and voice of God. A few minutes later she spoke of curiosity in her sermon. It was formed as the question of the morning and the interrogative hung in the air around her words. "How do we listen to the routine reading of a Scripture lesson in a worship setting? Do we bring imagination and intention to that moment of liturgy?" This is not a formula for listening as much as a glimpse into the process itself: imagination and intention in a spirit of curiosity. She was herself listening even as she spoke the words of a prepared sermon. Remarkable.

For many who read these words, her question is an important one because you often find yourself in settings where Scriptures (sacred writings) are read aloud. In our church we say words after the reading of Scripture such as "Hear what the Spirit is saying to God's people." Because I have been the one on the speaking side of the pulpit most of my life, I seem to need an extra nudge to listen with intentionality and imagination. I found it that day as I watched Dr. McDaniels listen to the text about which she was preaching. It was clear she had listened and listened still as her own words hung alive in the sanctuary.

Worship is active listening in the way we've talked about throughout this book. It is a response to the movement of God in our lives. It begins, as the ancients understood, in adoration. They started in a posture of listening adoration: "O come, let us worship and bow down, let us kneel before the LORD, our Maker" (Psalm 95:6). I love liturgy because it points me toward the living and speaking voice of God, Father, Son and Holy Spirit, and I am fed with soul nourishment by preaching that isn't timid about making heard the voice of Jesus. Liturgy comes from a word that means "the work of the people." Like spirituality in all of life, biblically informed worship insists on active attention to the person and character of the living God through the voice of Jesus. Why? There is no text more clear than Hebrews 1:

Long ago God spoke to our ancestors in many and various ways by the prophets, but in these last days he has spoken to us by a Son, whom he appointed heir of all things, through whom he also created the worlds. He is the reflection of God's glory and the exact imprint of God's very being, and he sustains all things by his powerful word. (Hebrews 1:1-3)

PRACTICE LISTENING: LISTENING TO A SERMON IN WORSHIP

Mars Hill Church in Michigan offers suggestions on how to listen to a sermon in worship. They offer a simple framework, a discipline for listening for the voice of God through the words of another.

- What words, phrases, or ideas did you connect with? Why?
- Was there anything that disturbed you or felt unsettling? Why?
- What did you hear that you want to know more about?
- Finish this sentence: If I take this seriously, then that would mean _____.
- What questions does this raise for you?
- If you had to draw what you just heard, what would you draw?[7]

nine

RABBI

Listening to the Life of Jesus

*[To teach] is to create a space in which
obedience to truth is practiced.*

PARKER PALMER

I LEARNED SPANISH AS A FRESHMAN in high school. Well,
that's an exaggeration of the word *learned*. It is more accurate to say I sat in classes where Spanish was spoken. I heard
sounds and recognized some of those sounds, but I learned
more about the language from working with Mexican Americans in my summer job at Portable Electric Tools, especially
from Pilar Pesina, my line boss. I learned grammar in the
classroom; I learned to speak Spanish in the factory. Similarly,
spirituality is learned best by immersion into a culture where
the language is spoken. It is cultivated in repeatable events and
life experiences, such as a daily commute, daily meals and the
liturgy of family practices. Otherwise we know rules of grammar,
isolated words, and fractured concepts, but we haven't learned

to speak the language of faith. It's one reason we are given Scripture—so we might listen to communities where faith was spoken. It is also the reason we learn best in *the company of others*. My time at the factory transformed my experience of learning from the schoolroom to all of life.

It might be accurate to say the same about Jesus. As a college student, I took a course commonly offered in Christian university education called Life and Teachings of Jesus. Codified around doctrinal content, the course was meant to be an introduction to how Jesus' life and teachings should be used to form the spirituality of young college students. More about his words than his life, the course gave me a lifetime full of ideas about what Jesus believed to be true. What I missed, however, is *how* Jesus himself learned to know and where his "classrooms" were. It is a breathtaking observation: the rabbi learned to listen. As a first-century Jew, Jesus was trained to listen in the various forms written about in this book. He knew the first words of creation in Genesis, the words of *Shema* and lament. He learned to listen to the narratives of his own people and the orienting words of the poetry of the psalms and the prophets. Jesus was a first-century teacher who gathered students (disciples), but he continued to learn to listen in the particularity of his own life experience. "And the Word became flesh and lived among us, and we have seen his glory, the glory as of a father's only son, full of grace and truth" (John 1:14). Jesus is the Word, the Logos, whom John says "became flesh and lived among us" in the particularity of his own life.

THE LIFE AND LEARNING OF JESUS

One way to think of the life and teaching of Jesus is to replace *teaching* with *learning* in the name of my college class: the life and *learning* of Jesus suggests that he himself practiced what he taught others, specifically to listen to the voice of God in all things and at all times. His classrooms were many and varied—indoors and out, formal and informal, planned and spontaneous. In cities and along the seaside, in boats and on mountain trails, in the city and in small towns, in worship and at tables, Jesus "became flesh and blood, and moved into the neighborhood" (John 1:14 *The Message*). He learned alone and with others but always, it seems, alert to a universe alive to the living presence and speaking voice of Abba, the God he would teach others to know, trust, love and obey.

It's not hard to walk the landscape of his first-century world and learn to listen from our teacher, Jesus. I want to live in that kind of world too—alert and leaning in for what might be revealed, spoken and made known. Jesus is the one God sent to us to give voice to the mind and heart of God. Active listening for the voice of God means, in part, listening to the words of Jesus in the Gospels. But that is not all we must listen to. Jesus resisted what philosophers might now call a "closed universe," where rational discourse, human thoughts and speech are all that exist. Jesus knew the universe instead to be a place alive with what Paul would later call "principalities and powers." Max Weber, a twentieth-century social theorist, said, "The fate of our times is characterized by rationalization and intellectualization and, above all, by the 'disenchantment of the world.'"[1] We have, in other words, decided the universe is no longer a place of enchantment, wonder, presence and voice. It isn't the universe Jesus found as he listened. Instead, it's a universe in which I am closed to what theologians call revelation, an unveiling or disclosure of the mind of God. Jesus believed differently and taught others to remain open to revelation; he lived alive and alert to

what he called the kingdom of God, a universe of revelation. I
contend the rabbi was himself a student of listening in many
classrooms. He lived what he taught: to listen in all things.

In Bethlehem: learning to listen in the household. The dramatic
doctrine of incarnation says that Jesus lived in time and space,
in other words, in a particular time and a specific location. That's
not an abstract or academic observation but rather something
that grounds Jesus' life in his own story. Jesus lived as a first-
century Jew, but that's not the end of it; his experience was located as well in a particular religious culture shaped by a very
specific political and social setting. Biblical teachings show he
was raised in the culture and life of his community, people
whose lives were marked by the liturgies, practices and torah
(way of life) of Jews living in the shadow of the Roman Empire.
His life and his own spirituality reflect the practices of first-
century Judaism: he prayed daily, observed weekly sabbath,
obeyed ceremonial and ritual torah, and honored the role of the
rabbi. He participated in the pilgrimage to Jerusalem for the
holy days. He doubtless became part of the synagogue as he
grew. His practices included reverence for sabbath, prayer, giving
of alms and fasting. Where did he learn these things? We could
call it the school of Mary and Joseph. Many of them were taught
in the home, which is the primary and foundational pillar for all
first-century Jewish spirituality.

Family shapes us and limits us. We are enculturated by
family history, culture and experience. The phone company
many years ago sponsored a series about how we are shaped by
such things. Its tagline was "You are where you were when."
You might want to read that again, out loud, slowly. Their
premise was that early identity is formed by early experiences
of time and location. I am the product of a mix of ethnic

Swedish Lutheran, Salvation Army, Conservative Baptist, American Baptist and now Anglican church life. My experience on the south side of Chicago in my earliest years was not duplicated in my wife's experience of early schooling in Seattle, eastern Washington, Missouri and Alabama.

Place matters. I grew up in suburban, mostly white schools in the fifties and sixties. Wendy lived in Alabama during Dr. King's march from Selma to Montgomery. My children's experience in school was in the eighties and nineties in urban Michigan and Washington State, small-town South Dakota and suburban Minnesota.

Time matters. Jesus grew up in an exclusive Jewish culture. He was raised to think in categories that I was not. His world was defined by a culture of the clean and unclean. There were insiders (Jews) and outsiders (Gentiles). It was a culture where women's lives were strictly defined by the household with a focus on "indoors" and family, while men were engaged in the community with an external focus. The synagogue was not for women; a *minion* or quorum of ten men composed the most important public schoolhouse for faith, but "women need not apply." There was a veil to separate them from the real "action" of the synagogue.

Some of Jesus' teachings and later practices are surprising, even shocking in light of his cultural training. He broke public rules of decorum as he spoke to women in public and included them in the study of theology. He entrusted the message of the resurrection—the most important message in human history—to the women who would carry the word to the others. Raised in a time of political resistance to Rome, he marginalized political resistance as he subverted it with teachings of an alternative kingdom, which he called the kingdom of heaven. But he learned important things in the school of Mary and Joseph. Luke tells us that "Mary treasured all these words and pondered them in her heart" (Luke 2:19). She alone knew the mystery of a birth initiated by the power of the Holy Spirit. Who better to teach Jesus about love, obedience and the mystery of God's presence? Perhaps of greatest importance is that he learned to pray. He understood life as a conversation with the Creator. He learned to order his life around the rhythms of God, which included time to stop (sabbath). He learned worship at home and in pilgrimages to the temple. Every Friday at sunset, he would join the family for a simple meal, candles and prayer. In the weekly *shabbat* he learned to stop work in order to remember God. He heard the stories of his people and knew himself to be part of a people with a history and experience of redemption. They spoke of "the mighty acts of God" and told the stories as their own, not as distant history but as the stories of themselves as the people of God.

> And when your children ask you, "What do you mean by this observance?" you shall say, "It is the Passover sacrifice to the LORD, for he passed over the houses of the Israelites in Egypt, when he struck down the Egyptians but spared our houses." And the people bowed down and worshiped. (Exodus 12:26-27)

First-century Jews understood their identity as people of *kadosh*, holy people set apart for a particular mission in the world. This also led to a society that defined the world as clean or unclean. He learned Torah (Scripture), which he recited daily in memorized oral discourse. And, I believe deeply, he learned that we do not come to faith alone.

In Jesus' household, the curriculum was God. "The LORD is our God, the LORD alone. You shall love the LORD your God with all your heart, and with all your soul, and with all your might" (Deuteronomy 6:5). It starts with God. It starts in a voice that speaks before we understand language. It starts in a voice that has been speaking long before we arrived on the scene. The timeline does not start here. The school of Joseph and Mary could well be designated the school of memory. "Remember the days of old, consider the years long past; ask your father, and he will inform you; your elders, and they will tell you" (Deuteronomy 32:7).

Every week the *shabbat* (sabbath) took place in the home. A time of prayer, yes, but also a time of leisurely feasting. Two instructions were given:

- *Zakhor* (Remember): "Remember the sabbath day, and keep it holy" (Exodus 20:8).

- *Shamor* (Observe): "Observe the sabbath day and keep it holy" (Deuteronomy 5:12).

Remember that God has been active in your life to give you political and religious freedom from Egypt. Observe the sabbath—practice it, do it, don't just talk about it. In the observation, the prayers passed on for generations include the following: prayer over the candles that are symbols of God's presence, prayer over the bread and the wine, and blessings over the children. Where are we formed spiritually? In practices such as these. To be blessed every single week of your childhood—it's overwhelming to think of the powerful teaching those moments provide.

Listening in the household is also about generations. I spent time one summer on short vacations with my children and two of my grandsons. Samuel was then only seven weeks old and chose not to go camping with us, but he did decide he needed to have an unexpected, week-long hospitalization, spinal tap and surgery. It also happened during that summer that we placed my father under Hospice care to wait out the days for his departure from us. Past, present and future were vividly conscious to me in that summer. I saw the past in the imminence of my father's passing, the present in all of us alive in this moment, and the future in the eyes of Benjamin, Andrew and Samuel. It's been said that a community that cares about future must care about education. If we care about future generations, we remember past generations and what they have to teach us, for the generations are teachers as no other voices can be. There is a currency of intellectual and spiritual capital found only in the stories of the past that precede this moment in history. Anyone who cares about the unfolding of generations invests in covenant with the future through the covenant in the past and the present. In my world I now carry the noble title of grandfather. Teaching my seven grandchildren will take a different shape than it did with my own three children, but I see and know the grand opportunities my wife and I will be given as grandparents in the households of our children. We will be able to say things with more clarity than our children can in certain moments. We will be heard differently because we are one generation removed from their parents.

Psalm 78 is relentless in noting the generational role played in faith development. Notice the statements highlighted below.

> Give ear, O my people, to my teaching;
> 　incline your ears to the words of my mouth.
> I will open my mouth in a parable;
> 　I will utter dark sayings from of old,

things that we have heard and known,
that our ancestors have told us.
We will not hide them from their children;
we will tell to the coming generation
the glorious deeds of the LORD, and his might,
and the wonders that he has done.

He established a decree in Jacob,
and appointed a law in Israel,
which he commanded our ancestors
to teach to their children;
that the next generation might know them,
the children yet unborn,
and rise up and tell them to their children,
so that they should set their hope in God,
and not forget the works of God,
but keep his commandments. (Psalm 78:1-7)

There are human voices, we are told, that will carry the divine voice to future generations. Listening is not only waiting for a revelation in new words but finding it in the voices of parents, grandparents, mentors, teachers and leaders who tell the next generation to remember what has already been heard.

In Nazareth: learning to listen in the community of others. Jesus' spiritual formation took him out of the home to another community, the synagogue in his hometown of Nazareth. There was a particular day when young Jesus stepped forward in the synagogue, was handed the scroll (Bible) and asked to interpret a text from Isaiah. What he said nearly incited a riot, but the ritual of the scroll is not to be bypassed too quickly. Jesus was shaped by a community who were people of a text. Torah (Scripture) was read in order to hear the continuing voice of a living God. In some cultural sense, Torah was held by the community itself and belonged to them as a whole more than to any one individual. In our culture it seems the opposite is true—if we are biblical people we tend to have our own canon of meaning, our own selection of texts that we prefer. Not so for Jesus. He knew himself shaped and formed by a community and the text that defined and empowered them. It happened when he matriculated at the Nazareth School.

Today we might say that Jesus showed up at church. Jesus went into the synagogue, respectful of authority, and received the word for the day—he was literally handed the text from the elders, those who held the authority for the traditions of the community. This is a powerful example on his part for his disciples. He received the scroll and thus submitted to the authority of the structures in which and from which he had learned faith. He received the scroll respectfully and functioned within the structure insofar as he could, within his own calling to his ministry and within his own conscience. Those things would lead him at other times to reject the abuse of power in the temple, but in Luke 2 the story starts with a common event: Scripture as a word of God was handed to Jesus by the previous generation. Some believe the synagogue was created after the exile to replace the temple. Synagogue was more than just a place; it was a way to restore connection to Torah.

Jesus took what the tradition gave him and then subverted it faithfully. He did not tell them only what they wished to hear; he went beyond their comfort level and spoke a truth they did not want to hear, in fact, a truth they were not ready to hear. And that is also instructive. Truth is not always like honey on our lips; it may taste or feel sweet, but it may have a strange and sour taste because it does not come only to confirm and comfort but to subvert and challenge. "Today this Scripture has been fulfilled in your hearing" (Luke 4:21): "The kingdom is here, the Messiah you have waited stands before you, embodied in an incarnate one, living in flesh in time and place." He was respectful, but he spoke truth that would lead to change. Jesus practiced his faith in community with others.

Exegesis, practiced properly, is biblical interpretation in the service of the Christian community of faith—to inform us, to inspire us, to correct our theological missteps and to propel us to serve the kingdom that Jesus proclaimed. There is an uninformed, misinformed or simply malformed practice of misreading the Bible called eisegesis. We take a text out of its context and attempt to let it say whatever fits our interest at the moment. My first and best teacher of exegesis was Berkley Michelson, who taught a class then called Biblical Prolegomena, a prologue to the study of Scripture. An excellent scholar and fine teacher of the text, he was also an apprentice of Jesus. Classes began with what I considered a "listening exegesis," in which we waited on the Spirit of God to open our ears to the voice of God. Michelson's Bible was a battered and worn Hebrew text held together with a rubber band. And always, his mind was tilted in a posture of listening—not only for grammar or vocabulary or historical and cultural meaning but for God to speak a word into the classroom. I remember a day when he asked me to read the text for the day and stopped me after a few phrases. "Please read that again, I don't think they got it right." And he told us how the Hebrew words meant something other than our standard biblical text had interpreted it. I was flabbergasted—he had just corrected the Bible!

So first-century Jews practiced their faith in conversation with Torah. Jesus was trained in a particular way of reading the

Bible of his community; he was trained in good exegesis of the
traditions that shaped culture and religion in his day. Tradition
is having a hard time of it these days. Dismissed by some as
modernist in a postmodern or post-Christian world, text is considered an anachronism. Scripture as authoritative text is replaced
by a random collection of my favorite writers, songs and poetry.
Rigorous, thoughtful, informed exegesis is too often replaced by
something less. We become like children staring at a handful of
stars on a dark night claiming we are astronomers. I work every
day with theologians, biblical scholars and exegetes who are
masterful students of the Word. They practice a craft that ac-
knowledges the Scripture we hold in our hands was written in
ancient forms of language in other eras of history in different
cultures, customs and in a geography that is entirely unlike Seattle in the twenty-first century. They read the ancient texts in
original languages and dig deeply as archaeologists into the ancient cultures to give informed meaning to what I read today.
Exegesis honors the traditions of the past and interprets in light
of the present. It is one of our most important ways to listen to
the voice of God. Reading Scripture with careful exegetical skill
is hard work. Perhaps that's why it seems to have fallen on hard
times in the life of the church. Without attention to the voices
of the past we can silence God's intentions for our communities.

Recently we talked about the culture of our graduate school
in a staff meeting. We intended to reclaim something called
"the Rule," which was an old document of our values. It was not
"the rules" but rather a set of intentions for how we would live
and work together in our mission. Our dean of students and
alumni, Paul Steinke, caught me completely off guard when he
said, "This document tells us the dreams an earlier generation
of this community had for us." Breathtaking! What we do in

community today gives shape to dreams for the community of future generations.

The Nazareth community was like that. There are specific edges to our faith: like Jesus, we are handed the scroll from the faith community; it is not ours to create as we wish. There are *givens* to Christian faith, a sense of *paralambano*, traditions passed on to us that define our spiritual truth. There are dreams others have for us and for the future, some we willingly accept and some we cannot; but faith is given and received within the community of the church as something passed on, handed down as a faith tradition.

In one of the strangely dramatic stories of Jesus' formation, he was "driven into the desert by the Holy Spirit" for an encounter that would shape his life. Some suggest this is a moment of clarification of the most essential leadership question: Who is in charge? Who sets the agenda? Jesus is not sent to the desert as punishment but to enter an experience he needed to shape his life and ministry. It is not a time for passivity on Jesus' part; it's an active encounter with God through the Holy Spirit.

IN THE DESERT

Henri Nouwen speaks of the desert experience in vivid terms:

> Solitude is the furnace of transformation. Without solitude we remain victims of our society and continue to be entangled in the illusions of the false self. Jesus himself entered into this furnace. There he was tempted with the three compulsions of the world: to be relevant ("turn stones into loaves"), to be spectacular ("throw yourself down"), and to be powerful ("I will give you all these kingdoms"). There he affirmed God as the only source of his identity

("you must worship the Lord your God and serve him alone"). Solitude is the place of the great struggle and the great encounter—the struggle against the compulsions of the false self, and the encounter with the loving God who offers himself as the substance of the new self.[2]

In the desert, Jesus learned and teaches us that God is the subject, the primary actor, in all spiritual life but especially in leadership. There is only one true leader and only one authentic gospel agenda: that which is given by the living Lord to an attentive church. God is the one who is alive, active, present and guiding. Colossians 1:17 confirms that in a single statement: "He himself is before all things, and in him all things hold together." Present-tense action by the cosmic Lord is the work of coherence—of holding "all things together." This is not a historical statement but a present action. Jesus Christ holds all things together. "He is the head of the body, the church . . . for in him all the fullness of God was pleased to dwell" (Colossians 1:18-19). History is saturated with a God presence and God action that shapes the agenda for any community.

I don't know if Jesus spoke aloud or was spoken to in oral sounds, but the desert is often the place for silence—terrifying silence, comforting silence, wild and ragged silence, or gentle silence, but listening silence just the same. It was, I am convinced, silence teeming with presence. Befriending the silence is another modality for hearing the voice of God—we wait, anticipate and continue to pay attention in the silence. Julian Treasure contrasts two forms of listening. Reductive listening, he says, is "listening for." It is a stereotypical male way of listening. We listen *for* the problem to be solved and immediately set to work on the solution. Expansive listening is "listening with." It is more commonly a female way of listening.[3] We listen *with* another person in relationship and curiosity. It is a listening that can wait for the presence of another to emerge. Some call it meditative or contemplative listening, others name it holy listening or even prayer; it is a way of life in which we actively listen for what God might reveal.

In the desert Jesus faced three tests that all had to do with agenda and methodology:

- Command stones to become bread—the temptation for immediacy, relevance or pragmatics.

- Throw yourself down from the Temple—the temptation for power.

- Worship Satan in order to be given all the kingdoms of the world—the temptation for avoidance of suffering.

To all three tests, Jesus' response was one of clarifying reality:

- One lives by the Word of God.

- One does not test the Lord.

- God alone is to be worshiped.

The central response of Jesus in each case is to state in startling simplicity: God is the initiating and sustaining source. Matthew is insistent that Jesus' enrollment in the desert school of solitude was God-initiated: "Then Jesus was led up by the Spirit into the wilderness to be tempted by the devil" (Matthew 4:1). This was not a random or serendipitous occasion but a God-initiated, God-intended, God-designed encounter. Jesus might have heard God's voice in ways none of us ever will but in this desert school he didn't seem to refer to any private revelation; he says to the adversary, "God has already spoken in the words of the Scripture of my people. We live by those words. We listen.

We shape our lives on God's word, God's intentions and God's exclusivity." It is a remarkable moment in which Jesus practices the revelation learned over a lifetime. Jesus' response was not a new insight, idea or "word from the Lord"; it was listening to what he already knew. In the company of solitude Jesus never was alone. He showed what he already knew from a lifetime of listening to Scripture. His listening was formed by hearing Scripture read and practiced by mindfulness to what he heard. In our solitude it is time to practice what we already know.

PRACTICE LISTENING: IN THE COMPANY OF SILENCE

"In the morning, while it was still very dark, he got up and went out to a deserted place, and there he prayed" (Mark 1:35). We often superficially, I believe, use this text as *the* case for having a time of morning devotions and miss the deeper meaning that is modeled for us in this text: Jesus needed silence in order to listen to God. Jesus' ministry is one of responsive listening to the Father in the empowerment of the Holy Spirit. He couldn't always get that in the busyness of the business. He couldn't always get that in the noise and distractions of the rhythms of daily life. Sometimes he had to stop in order to listen.

Mother Teresa said, "I always begin my prayer in silence, for it is in the silence of the heart that God speaks. God is the friend of silence, so we need to listen. For, it is not what we say, but what God says to us and through us that matters. Prayer feeds the soul—as blood is to the body, prayer is to the soul and it brings us closer to God."[4] I have reflected often on that simple statement and the life that surrounded it. She lived her life of prayer in cities where there is much noise, chaos and distractions. She followed the wisdom of Catherine of Sienna, the fourteenth-century Italian mystic who grew up in a household of twenty-five children. Silence was hard to come by! But she said she believed we have a cell within each of us where we can go to be with God in prayer. It is to that cell we must return every day.[5]

There's a lot of noise and distraction in all of our lives. So we are taught as Jesus learned to befriend silence. In silence and solitude, we can be honest and set aside any need for performance for others. It intrigues me in the Mark text that Jesus hid so well the disciples had to "hunt" for him. He didn't just step into the next room; he went to a place to be alone with God. It was a discipline he had developed over his life: he learned how to focus in active prayer. Listening begins with finding a quiet center within.

Through the centuries many teachers have understood the physicality of silence. It doesn't always require a hut in the Himalayas without people, sound or distractions, but it often begins by quieting your body through deep and slow breathing. As we quiet our bodies, our spirits will become more receptive to listen. Richard Foster draws a distinction that should not be missed: "Whenever the Christian idea of meditation is taken seriously, there are those who assume it is synonymous with the concept of meditation centered in Eastern religions. In reality, the two ideas stand worlds apart. Eastern meditation is an attempt to empty the mind; Christian meditation is an attempt to fill the mind. The two ideas are quite different."[6] Practicing silence is a way to create a free and open space for listening—it is hospitality for the presence and voice of God's Spirit.

ten

ACCENT

Diverse Languages of the Soul

*The Bible makes it clear that every time
that there is a story of faith, it is completely
original. God's creative genius is endless.*

EUGENE PETERSON

W E ALL NEED COMMUNITY, what some might even call a "tribe." In the end, our listening intends to create what Wendell Berry calls "membership," by which he means that we are known by others and find our identity in the context of those relationships. Sharon Daloz Parks says, "We need a place or places of dependable connection, where we have a keen sense of the familiar: ways of knowing and being that anchor us in a secure sense of belonging and social cohesion."[1] First-century Jews had a highly developed network of belonging that formed them, created safety and provided a space for their development of emerging generations. But we all need "otherness" as well as tribe. The first century was racially, economically and socially fragmented. Jesus became a rabbi for otherness in that first-century culture.

The troubling truth of Jesus is that he didn't stay in the crèche of Luke 2. He grew up and walked into the neighborhoods of an oppressed nation. The troubling truth of Jesus is not the mystery of angels, magi and a stable but that he moved into the neighborhood where we live. The troubling truth of Jesus is that he moved beyond the neighborhoods of people who look like me and live as I do. The troubling truth of Jesus is that he learned to listen for God's voice in unexpected voices and surprising places.

That is the narrative of Jesus' visit to Samaria. According to John, Jesus "*had* to go through Samaria" (John 4:4, emphasis added), but not because the highway required his journey there; as it turned out, Jesus went to Samaria for another surprise encounter with listening, this time with someone a good rabbi would normally avoid. She was a woman of Samaria considered of mixed race in a culture that valued lineage and cultural purity. She is a symbol of differentness or otherness. In Jesus' world, Jews and Samaritans did not mix; in fact, the Jewish historian Josephus even speaks of violence between these two groups. Look carefully at the story in John's Gospel and you will see the discomfort of the disciples, who clearly wanted Jesus to move on from this "unclean" woman and her culture.

SCHOOLED BY OTHERNESS

The Samaritan woman offered Jesus' disciples an opportunity for schooling in "otherness." His friends were scandalized by Jesus' disregard for social conventions as he spoke to a woman in public, something rabbis did not do; as he spoke theology to a woman, something men in Israel were not to do; as he allowed himself to be seen in public with a woman who was of the

Samaritan population, a group despised by pure-blood Jews, something Jews did not do. In the end, he spent two days in that Samaritan village, immersing his disciples in a cultural encounter for which they were not prepared and an encounter with otherness. *Otherness* simply means people who are different than those with whom we identify, affiliate or associate, people different from our tribe or "membership." Otherness may be racial, but increasingly it is economic and cultural as well. In some neighborhoods it is religious, but for many of us it is political, ideological and theological. We live as segregated theologically as did Jesus and Paul in their world defined for them into the categories of clean and unclean. There were Jews and there were Gentiles (pagan). In the church today that division is often drawn around sexuality or politics. We affiliate only with those with whom we agree on particular issues such as sexuality, immigration, economic policies and worldview. In my school years my life was defined by the treatment of my special-need brother who experienced the violence of brain damage in the final hours before his birth. Those few hours changed his life and all of ours as his "otherness" became a factor for social awkwardness, rejection and even public ridicule by some. Even in an affluent and educated community, we experienced the bias and rejection of someone often labeled as a "retard." He was different, and he is still, but most never get to know him for the gentle soul he is because they are unwilling to listen to the differentness.

We aren't much good at listening to otherness—different languages, worldviews, ages, genders, sexualities, abilities, demographics, religions or philosophies. We are tribal in the best sense of the word, I suppose. Like my immigrant grandparents who found their way to Swedish-speaking communities in Chicago, we find those who share our beliefs, visions and dreams for life. So we live and worship with those who are like-minded. But we are tribal in the worst sense of the word too. We believe or act as if our ideas are right, our ways are the best, and our practices set us apart and above others. My father once told me that the United States was the most beautiful and best place on earth. Ironically, in his life, he never traveled beyond the borders of this country. Grandma Liljedahl talked about her attempt to speak "American," as she called it, and rued the fact that hers was always "broken English." Without differentness, otherness, diversity or simple exposure to other people, we remain in gated communities of limited thought and tribal views. For many of us, education is the pathway to new ideas, new accents and new ways. I remember an early assault on my religious views in a book with the startling title *Your God Is Too White*. It catapulted me back to a memory as a young boy. We lived by then in the western suburbs of Chicago but supported a church on the west side of Chicago through our "home missions" program. On a winter's Sunday afternoon, we drove into the city to our "sister church" to listen to Pastor Lloyd Lindo preach. I stood in a dark hallway at Keystone Baptist Church in complete bewilderment and confusion. I stared at a painting hung on the foyer wall that we too had in the entryway of our suburban home. It was a painting of Jesus, but in the church foyer it was all wrong! Jesus didn't have the white face he did in my living room; Jesus' face was black. I was so troubled I told my mother that night that something was wrong in their congregation—Jesus wasn't like that, why didn't they understand? I know now that God showed up in my life in the voice and face of those who did not sound or look like I expected them to be.

Years later, I sat in a sixth-floor classroom on the north side of Chicago with students in a class on urban ministry and sociology. Chad said to me with trembling voice and emotions, "How could they lie to me? I grew up trusting my church. Why did I have to come to the inner city to learn that God cares for justice, the poor and oppression? Why didn't they tell me the whole story?" And the answer is simple: we do not know the whole story alone; *together* we hear the whole story. Today there is rapid growth of the church in the Global South even as the church in Europe and North America seems to drift toward irrelevance. And yet, there are movements of growth of the church in neighborhoods in new forms and new structures that have heard a larger vision for the kingdom of God. *Together we hear the whole story; together we tell the whole story.*

Diverse Languages of the Soul

I teach spirituality to graduate students, pastors and leaders. I am an educated, white male who is an introvert. I am both an intellectual and a practitioner; I am not a mystic, although at times in my life I wanted to be. Not everyone I teach fits that description. In fact, many of the millennials I now teach aren't at all motivated by the study of Scripture, spirituality and faith in ways that are most comfortable for me. It has happened in the classroom that someone will ask a question that seems to have no connection with anything I have just taught. Is that because they are especially unsuited for the course or is something different at work? We come to faith in a diversity of pathways. We learn Jesus in a diversity of ways. We come to know God in ways that seem more hard-wired into our personalities and nature than in our preferred ways of learning.

Learning to listen to God also means learning to listen to those who listen to God in ways that are unfamiliar or just different than my way. Whole traditions, denominations, churches, and communities have been formed based on a single privileged way of listening. Another way of listening invites us to ask bigger questions: How do we experience God's presence? Do we know God through the mind (rationalism, thinking) or through the heart (feelings, emotions)? Entire denominations are based on a singular answer to that question. Later monastics identified what can be called "the paradox of the two ways." They accepted multiple answers to the questions above rather than one.

- God is known in the positive language of presence; this is called the *kataphatic*.

- And God is known in the negative language of absence; this is called *apophatic*.

In kataphatic spirituality (with images) we imagine God in symbols, metaphors, rituals, worship, seeing, tasting, incense, candles and sounds. Historically a great deal of Protestant spirituality is what may be called the *via positiva*, or positive way. But it is not the only way. In apophatic spirituality there is an emphasis on passivity, receptivity and detachment from the world, what is called the *via negativa*. Apophatic prayer is primarily learning to empty the mind and heart of all images and know God in the surrender to unknowing. The goal is to seek mystical union with God. Kataphatic traditions choose instead to affirm or celebrate images, symbols and human words. This tradition doesn't say that God is only knowable in icons or human words, but that they are containers for God's presence. The goal is to evoke and experience God's love and presence. Simply stated, kataphatic prayer uses words, Scripture icons, songs and symbols; apophatic is prayer without words and images. Do we know God intellectually or emotionally, with symbols or without, through contemplation or action, by prayer or by action? In the world of computer logic, data is processed through two digits of binary language, which is ironically also called machine language. Binary logic says we must choose between two answers: either head or heart, cognitive ways of knowing or affective means. Machine language, however, is not the language of the soul. Some of us are wired, we might believe, for one way instead of the other. Jesus experienced the presence of God in both ways—in the desert without food and at the table with bread; in isolation, silence, and solitude and in the joy of children at play. Listening comes in many forms, some because of our natural proclivity for a familiar practice and some because we are driven into a place of isolation, silence and solitude.

There is a diversity of forms, practices, and modes of spirituality. Spirituality has been splintered by church history as denominations, theologies and spiritual teachers declared the priority of one particular form of spirituality over others. Richard Foster will be remembered for his insistence on prayer and spiritual practices, but I believe his greatest gift to us was in his book *Streams of Living Water*, in which he describes six forms of spirituality. Each grows out of a particular tradition with particular exemplars but together show us the depths of the spiritual life in their wholeness.

- Contemplative traditions are prayer filled and emphasize the meditative, monastic journey inward.

- Holiness traditions emphasize what is often called the deeper life that reflects the glory of God. It adds an emphasis on purity and a disciplined life.

- Charismatic traditions bring special focus to the work of the Holy Spirit, especially through spiritual gifts or charisms.

- Social justice traditions are what Chad was looking for—faith that is prophetic and involved in acts of justice, compassion and movements that address systemic evil and oppression in all forms.

- Evangelical traditions are Word-centered, with a strong reliance on biblical truth in propositional forms; they are highly evangelistic and strong on apologetics (a defense of the biblical text and its meaning).

- Incarnational traditions hold to a view that God is revealed in sacraments (sacred acts of Eucharist, baptism, confession, last rites); they are highly liturgical and highlight the arts and cultural engagement.[2]

FOR THE SAKE OF OTHERS

There is a preference for the mystical in North American culture these days. Where many forms of social action once seemed to dominate the landscape of Christian spirituality, now mystical forms seem to lead the charge. From yoga to practices of Eastern religions, silent retreats and daily silence, many have turned toward the mystical as their dominant spiritual practices. It was not so for Jesus.

An active teacher, preacher, healer and rabbinic leader, Jesus' practices were many and varied. Silence, solitude and quiet were necessary parts of his spirituality but so too were practices of the shared meal, corporate worship, storytelling, reading Torah, fasting and an active daily practice of walking as his common mode of transportation. I would add journaling, generous giving of time and money, study, laying on of hands, anointing with oil, and the sacraments of the Lord's Table and baptism. One final spiritual discipline to add to the suggestive list above is service.

Too easily forgotten in our hunger for spiritual experience is that there is a kingdom outcome to all spiritual growth. Jesus came to seek and to save others and sent his own followers to go "and make disciples of all nations, baptizing them in the name of the Father and of the Son and of the Holy Spirit, and teaching them to obey everything that I have commanded you" (Matthew 28:19-20). The early Christians defined themselves as those sent to give witness to what they had seen of Jesus, who was anointed, he said, "to bring good news to the poor . . . to proclaim release to the captives and recovery of sight to the blind, to let the oppressed go free, to proclaim the year of the Lord's favor" (Luke 4:18-19).

Meditation is not meant to lead to narcissistic self-indulgence but to motivate outward to service to others. The contemplative experience of silence and solitude is also not merely for private delight but to help us see where God is present to the world and calling us to join at the places of the world's great needs. Honest prayer for the one will always lead to prayers of intercession for others. It is the nature of drawing close to the presence and voice of God—like a centrifugal force that moves you outward from the center toward the world. Centripetal force draws you inexorably to the self; it is not the spirituality of Christlikeness found in Scripture. The sacrificial Christ is the template for those who serve as they lead, love and live in community with others.

I just finished a fascinating book by Daniel James Brown titled *The Boys in the Boat*. It is the story of the University of Washington eight-man rowing team that competed in 1936 in Nazi Germany for the Olympic gold medal. The book describes how ordinary individuals are formed into an extraordinary team with excellent coaching, equipment, mechanics and skill, but I was captivated by the need for mental focus and attention. Until this book, I knew nothing about rowing as a sport and even less about the demanding training, grueling physical exertion and disciplined mental stamina required of the athletes. One year a surprising freshman team began to outrun the veterans ahead of them. Sometimes disciplined, sometimes sloppy, distracted and inept, they found ways to win. At one point they created a mantra their coxswain chanted as they rowed: "M-I-B, M-I-B, M-I-B!" It meant "Mind in the boat," and was meant to remind the oarsman "he must keep his mind focused on what is happening inside the boat. His whole world must shrink down to the small space within the gun whales. He must maintain a singular focus on the rower just ahead of him and the voice of the coxswain calling out commands."[3]

Their simple discipline accentuates what I mean by a spirituality of listening: pay attention, focus, notice, discern, attend, be aware—and do it in the company of others. These young oarsmen cared deeply about their sport and competed with skill and distinction. But the glory and extraordinary moment of winning the Olympic gold came only because they paid attention in the ordinary days of practice in rain and sun, heat and cold, in season and out. Their time in the boat trained them through attention to hear the directions of the coxswain calling to them above the roar of the waves.

Jesus was schooled in prayer. He prayed daily as a faithful Jew would pray. He prayed ritualistically at table worship, at home, on the sabbath, in the temple and in the synagogue. But here we see him step away from the rituals of prayer in order to enter a "lonely place" for private prayer. I wonder if the loneliness was in Jesus and not only in the isolation of the location.

I would like to have listened in to Jesus at the schoolhouse on the mountain.

PRACTICE LISTENING: M-I-B

Listening in the classroom of Jesus' life is a way to remind us to listen to the many classrooms of our own lives. We are always in the place of learning whether we are mindful or not. Practicing M-I-B involves reading the timeline of your life as it unfolds and develops. It requires intention, attention and contemplative listening.

Create a timeline of the past half decade of your life and list the major events (new job, marriage, first child, illness, death of parent). On another horizontal line, write a descriptive word that identifies the meaning you attach to the event (*anticipation, fulfillment, delight, weariness, ambivalence, grief*). Now take sticky notes and write on them as follows: high points, low points, turning points. Attach the notes below the timeline and descriptors.

Stand back from work and look at the past years as an unfolding story. What do you see when you pay attention to "what's in the boat"? Are there surprise connections you didn't notice before? Where were the turning points? What made them more than just a high point or low point? What changed after the turning points?

Now you are ready to look ahead. Create another timeline across the top of a new page. Begin to list your dreams for yourself, your family, your work and your relationships. On another line begin to jot down descriptive words to answer this question: if nothing changes from today, what will my life be in three years, five years and ten years?

Now take sticky notes and begin to create an action plan for your future.

RESURRECTION

Listening to Hope

It's the very nature of wonder to catch us off guard,
to circumvent expectations and assumptions. Wonder can't
be packaged, and it can't be worked up. It requires some
sense of being there and some sense of engagement.

EUGENE PETERSON

◇◆◇

I HAVE BEEN TO EASTER most of my life. I have experienced Easter all of my life in ministry, often in lofty terms about the resurrection of the body at some moment in the future. Often in the confusion of those who discovered the moment first, the women who returned to the disbelief of the men. Often in the music, the ineffable music of hymns and spiritual songs. Often in the singing of Handel's Messiah. This year, though, I found myself at the beach for breakfast. Wendy has an allergy to lilies, and our church likes a lot of lilies on Easter morning. So we found our way to a picnic table at Fay Bainbridge State Park, on the beach of Puget Sound, for breakfast, reading and prayer. We had a view of the Seattle skyline off in the distance to the east, the Olympic mountains to the north and the Cascades in full view in front of us. Better than a sermon on resurrection, some might say because it wasn't contained in a building. That's what struck me that day—after resurrection Jesus also moved to the beach where his new resurrected body could no longer be contained. Resurrection is an event in history; Jesus returned to the disciples and made them breakfast at the beach. Fish and bread, no doubt, but it wasn't a vision for the disciples in a disembodied way; they received food from the hands that prepared it for them.

I used to think Easter and resurrection are hard concepts for people to accept. Jesus is alive and well on Friday, dead on Saturday, and pops back to life in a now-empty grave on Sunday morning. It seems too neat and orderly, fanciful and a bit scripted for prime time. A problem needs a heroic solution, and resolution comes three days later, just in time. I don't think it is as hard for people to accept as it is to get the church to believe. Many of us are longing for the miraculous presence of God. We are desperate, some of us, for deliverance and rescue; we know we need saving. So we look to a time and place where that happened, and we are bold to claim the hope that resurrection brings. Hope when the only thing staring you in the face is death. Trust in something more when there is nothing left to believe. Anticipation of life after what seems like the end.

However, hope is not an ethereal concept of optimism based on certain rescue. In *Abba's Child: The Cry of the Heart for Intimate Belonging* Brennan Manning wrote, "For me the most radical demand of Christian faith lies in summoning the courage to say yes to the present risenness of Jesus Christ."[1] Listening requires courage. It may be something we long for, but it doesn't

come easily. Have you ever listened to the words from the disciples when the women return with good news? In Luke's
Gospel it says it sounded to them like an idle tale, and they did
not believe the words of the women. That which they should
have heard most elatedly they did not believe. What they should
have learned in all of their time with Jesus they now thought
was an idle tale. The most repeated reaction to appearances of
the resurrected Jesus was fear. Rather than welcome Jesus back
as if they expected his return, the disciples were afraid, so Jesus
showed up and made them breakfast. He let them touch his
body, the piercings and the wounds. They heard the timbre of
his voice and only then slowly came to a place of belief.

It didn't come naturally to them and it doesn't come easily to
us. We have all been disappointed by optimism, damaged by
hope and deceived by our dreams. When I first heard the following words of Cornel West, they took my breath away. They
are raw and honest and touched the hunger of my soul.

> Hope and optimism are different. Optimism tends to be
> based on the notion that there's enough evidence out there
> to believe things are gonna be better, much more rational,
> deeply secular, whereas hope looks at the evidence and says,
> "It doesn't look good at all. Doesn't look good at all. Gonna
> go beyond the evidence to create new possibilities based
> on visions that become contagious to allow people to
> engage in heroic actions always against the odds, no guar-
> antee whatsoever." That's hope. I'm a prisoner of hope,
> though. Gonna die a prisoner of hope.[2]

My office has what I call a one-sixth view of Mount Rainier,
some ninety miles away. If I lean forward and tilt my head just
right I can see half of the mountain. Except there are clouds

some days, rain some days—it is Seattle, after all. Out the same window I can see two-hundred-foot-tall orange derricks that get loaded on the container ships to sail to Japan. Some days all I see is gray, driving rain or the offices of the Port of Seattle and Starbucks and the marina and an empty pier and road construction. But I have learned to train my beliefs that there is a stunning, unrelentingly beautiful 14,410-foot glaciated mountain there. Even when I do not see. Even when I forget to see. Even when I am caught up in my own small self. Even when I live in the worry and fear and anxieties of my responsibilities and my life. Even when I lose anything like natural optimism or confidence—even then the mountain is there and alive and changing and persists outside of my awareness of it.

That's why I return to the schoolhouse of resurrection on the beach every year. I come back to Easter because there is something here I can find nowhere else. I too am going to die a prisoner of hope. I don't claim that it's easy. I don't pretend that listening comes easily either. But at the end of the day I dare to believe we are alive in a universe that is alive with the presence and voice of the living God. As Annie Dillard wrote, "The least we can do is try to be there."[3]

ACKNOWLEDGMENTS

H OW DO YOU STOP A LIST of thanks to those who are
your teachers? It's easy enough to start, but to finish?
That's a different thing. My teachers have included those who
have been called to a profession: Doc Dalton, Garth Rosell,
Dan Erwin, Eugene Peterson and Tom Groome. Some teachers
have been colleagues at The Seattle School willing to walk
alongside me in the faltering steps of my "new" careers as dean
and president: Phil, Cathy, Paul and Derek, trustees, faculty,
and the best academic staff anywhere.

Dan, you pushed me to write again through hyperbole, per-
sistence and graceful humor.

Cindy Bunch, my editor for all of my books since 1995: your
patience with me has been gracious, and you have made me a
better writer than I could be otherwise.

To "Dotty," who has listened to my ideas and cheered me on
with encouragement. "Your stocks are up, today."

To Brennan, who helped me believe in myself again.

Eugene: your teachings have troubled me and nourished me
since I read your first book in 1981.

To my family, who teaches me every day: Kevin and Allison,
Sloane and Laine, Keri and Jon, Benjamin and Andrew, Kristoffer and Bethany, Samuel, Luke and Zachary Charles.

NOTES

CHAPTER 1: RESONANCE

[1]Wendell Berry, *Jayber Crow: The Life Story of Jayber Crow, Barber of the Port William Membership, as Written by Himself* (Washington, DC: Counterpoint, 2000), 29.

[2]Eugene Peterson, *The Jesus Way: A Conversation on the Ways That Jesus Is the Way* (Grand Rapids: Eerdmans, 2007), 37.

[3]Stephen Glazier, *Random House Word Menu* (New York: Ballantine, 1997).

[4]John Calvin, *Commentary on Genesis, Argumentum*, CO 22.8d, CTS I:57, 60. Emphasis added.

[5]Berry, *Jayber Crow*, 131.

[6]Ibid., 132.

[7]Ibid.

CHAPTER 2: FIRST WORDS

[1]Eugene Peterson, *Subversive Spirituality* (Grant Rapids: Eerdmans, 1997), 21, 23.

[2]John Irving, *A Prayer for Owen Meany* (New York: William Morrow, 1989), 1.

[3]Brennan Manning, *Ruthless Trust: The Ragamuffin's Path to God* (New York: HarperCollins, 2000), 6.

[4]Belden Lane, *Ravished Beauty: The Surprising Legacy of Reformed Spirituality* (New York: Oxford University Press, 2011).

[5]Helmut Thielicke, *How the World Began* (Cambridge: Lutterworth, 1964), 19, emphasis added.

[6]Barbara Brown Taylor, *Leaving Church: A Memoir* (New York: HarperCollins, 2006), 79-80.

[7]Kathleen Norris, *The Quotidian Mysteries: Laundry, Liturgy, and "Women's Work"* (New York: Paulist Press, 1998).

[8]Wendell Berry, *Jayber Crow: The Life Story of Jayber Crow, Barber of the Port

William Membership, as Written by Himself (Washington, DC: Counterpoint, 2000), 5.

9 Thomas H. Groome, *Sharing Faith: A Comprehensive Approach to Religious Education and Pastoral Ministry: The Way of Shared Praxis* (San Francisco: HarperSanFrancisco, 1991), 9.

10 See www.ugrad.cs.ubc.ca/~cs344/2013W1/tutorials/additionalMaterials /T03_HEAR_model.pdf.

Chapter 3: Household

1 Quoted in Belden Lane, *Ravished by Beauty: The Surprising Legacy of Reformed Spirituality* (New York: Oxford University Press, 2011), 68.

2 Annie Dillard, *Pilgrim at Tinker Creek*, quoted in *The Norton Book of Nature Writing*, ed. Robert Finch and John Elder (New York: W. W. Norton, 1990), 821.

3 Mary Oliver, *The House Light* (Boston: Beacon, 1990).

4 Lane, *Ravished by Beauty*, 216.

5 Thomas Merton, quoted in Annie Dillard, *Pilgrim at Tinker Creek* (New York: HarperCollins, 1974), 268.

6 Barbara Brown Taylor, *The Preaching Life* (Boston: Cowley, 1993), 15.

7 Andrew Greeley, *Andrew Greeley's Chicago* (Chicago: Contemporary, 1989), frontispiece.

8 Seth Horowitz, "The Science and Art of Listening," *The New York Times*, November 9, 2012, www.nytimes.com/2012/11/11/opinion/sunday/why-listening-is-so-much-more-than-hearing.html?_r=2&amp.

9 See www.age-of-the-sage.org/historical/biography/confucius.html.

10 Quoted in Lane, *Ravished by Beauty*, 72.

11 Ibid., 9.

12 Margaret Guenther, *Holy Listening: The Art of Spiritual Direction* (Lanham, MD: Rowman & Littlefield, 1992), 71.

13 Abraham Heschel, "Shabbat as a Sanctuary in Time," My Jewish Learning website, www.myjewishlearning.com/practices/Ritual/Shabbat_The _Sabbath/Themes_and_Theology/Sanctuary_in_Time.shtml.

Chapter 4: Surrounded by Sound

1 Julian Treasure, "How to Speak so That People Want to Listen," TED Talk, available at www.ted.com/talks/Julian_treasure_how_to_speak_so_that _people_want_to_listen.

[2]Ibid.

[3]Margaret Guenther, *Wisdom Distilled in the Daily: Living the Rule of St Benedict Today* (San Francisco: Harper & Row, 1990).

[4]Anonymous, *The Cloud of Unknowing*, cited in Bernard McGinn, *Essential Writings of Christian Mysticism* (New York: Random House, 2006), 264.

[5]See the translation of Deuteronomy 6:4 at www.jewfaq.org/prayer/shema .htm.

[6]Eugene H. Peterson, *Eat This Book: A Conversation in Spiritual Theology* (Grand Rapids: Eerdmans, 2006), 17.

[7]Thomas Merton, *New Seeds of Contemplation* (New York: New Directions Books, 1961), 14.

[8]Joan Chittister, *Wisdom Distilled from the Daily* (San Francisco: HarperSanFrancisco, 1990), 34.

[9]Sharon Daloz Parks, *Big Questions, Worthy Dreams: Mentoring Emerging Adults in Their Search for Meaning, Purpose, and Faith* (San Francisco: Jossey-Bass, 2011), 198-202.

[10]Will Willimon and Stanley Hauerwas, *Resident Aliens: A Provocative Christian Assessment of Culture and Ministry for People Who Know Something Is Wrong* (Nashville: Abingdon, 1989), 103.

[11]See www.shalem.org/index.php/resources/quotations/41-quotations/64-qu otations?tmpl=component&print=1&page=.

[12]Ibid.

[13]Ibid.

[14]Ibid.

[15]Thomas R. Kelly, *A Testament of Devotion* (San Francisco: HarperSanFrancisco, 1992), 3.

[16]Julian Treasure, "Five Ways to Listen Better," TED Talk, available at www .ted.com/talks/julian_treasure_5_ways_to_listen_better/transcript ?language=en.

[17]Summary available at *Inspired Blog*, "5 Ways to Listen Better—Julian Treasure," entry by Shobhit Chugh, May 6, 2012, http://shobhitchugh .blogspot.com/2012/05/5-ways-to-listen-better-julian-treasure.html.

CHAPTER 5: STORY

[1]Gary Vandenbos, ed., *The APA Dictionary of Psychology* (Washington, DC: American Psycological Assocation, 2006), 542.

[2]Interview with Dr. Dan Allender and Cathy Loerzel.

[3]Dan Allender, "To Be Told,"The Allender Center, http://theallendercenter .org/conferences/to-be-told.

[4]Interview with Dr. Dan Allender and Cathy Loerzel.

[5]Dan Allender, *To Be Told* (Colorado Springs: Waterbrook, 2006), 11.

[6]Ibid., 41-48.

[7]Frederick Buechner, *The Sacred Journey* (San Francisco: Harper & Row, 1982), 1.

[8]Ibid.

[9]Paula D'Arcy, quoted in Richard Rohr, *Falling Upward* (San Francisco: Jossey-Bass, 2011), 151.

[10]Ibid., p. xxx.

[11]Eugene Peterson, *Leap Over a Wall: Earthy Spirituality for Everyday Christians* (San Francisco: HarperSanFrancisco, 1997), 6.

[12]Wendell Berry, *Jayber Crow: The Life Story of Jayber Crow, Barber of the Port William Membership, as Written by Himself* (Washington, DC: Counterpoint, 2000), frontispiece.

[13]Melanie Tem, quoted by Suzanne Castle and Andra Moran, *Brim: Creative Overflow in Worship Design* (St. Louis: Chalice Press, 2013), 63.

[14]Allender Center Lecture by Cathy Loerzel.

[15]T. S. Eliot, "Ash Wednesday," in *T. S. Eliot: Collected Poems 1909–1962* (Orlando: Harcourt Brace, 1963).

[16]Howard Thurman, *Disciplines of the Spirit* (Richmond, IN: Friends United Press, 1963), 96.

CHAPTER 6: TRAJECTORIES

[1]Quoted in Paul Elie, *An American Pilgrimage* (New York: Farrar, Straus & Giroux, 2003), 265.

[2]Walter Brueggemann, *The Message of the Psalms* (Minneapolis: Fortress, 2002), 9-11.

[3]Flannery O'Connor, *Mystery and Manners* (New York: Farrar, Straus & Giroux, 1961), 112.

[4]Wendell Berry, *Jayber Crow: The Life Story of Jayber Crow, Barber of the Port William Membership, as Written by Himself* (Washington, DC: Counterpoint, 2000), 132.

[5]Dr. Brandon Walker, lecture at The Seattle School of Theology & Psychology.

[6]N. T. Wright, *The Case for the Psalms: Why They Are Essential* (New York: HarperCollins, 2011), 21.

[7]Alonzo Johnson, *Good News for the Disinherited: Howard Thurman on Jesus of Nazareth and Human Liberation* (Lanham, MD: University Press of America, 1997), 71.

[8]Barbara Brown Taylor, *Leaving Church: A Memoir of Faith* (New York: HarperCollins, 2006), 26, emphasis added.

[9]Abraham Heschel, *Man Is Not Alone: A Philosophy of Religion* (New York: Farrar, Straus & Giroux, 1976).

[10]Linford Detweiler, "What I'll Remember Most," *Ohio* by Over the Rhine (2003). Lyrics available at http://overtherhine.com/albums/ohio.

[11]Anne Lamott, *Traveling Mercies* (New York: Pantheon, 1999), 100.

[12]From www.awakechurch.org/auroracommons.

[13]Meister Eckhart, quoted in August Truk, "A Leadership Lesson from Meister Eckhart," Forbes.com, August 5, 2011, www.forbes.com/sites /augustturak/2011/08/05/a-leadership-lesson-from-meister-eckhart.

[14]Adapted from "The Prayer of Examen," Mars Hill Bible Church, http:// marshill.org/pdf/sp/PrayerOfExamenLong.pdf.

CHAPTER 7: HEARTBREAK

[1]Leonard Cohen, "Anthem," *The Future* (Columbia, 1992). See lyrics at www .metrolyrics.com/anthem-lyrics-leonard-cohen.html.

[2]Sue Monk Kidd, *The Invention of Wings* (London: Headline Publishing Group, 2014), 14.

[3]See www.bartleby.com/73/1995.html.

[4]Dan Allender, "The Hidden Hope of Lament," *Mars Hill Review*, 1994, 25-38.

[5]Ibid.

[6]*Harry Potter and the Prisoner of Azkaban*, dir. Alfonso Cuaròn (Warner Bros., 2004).

[7]Alan Jones, *Passion for Pilgrimage: Notes for the Journey Home* (Harrisburg, PA: Morehouse, 2000), 113.

[8]Walter Brueggemann, *The Message of the Psalms* (Minneapolis: Augsburg, 1984), 52.

[9]Ibid., 53.

[10]Ibid.

CHAPTER 8: WHAT WE DON'T WANT TO HEAR

[1]Walter Brueggemann, *Words That Linger, Texts That Explode: Listening to Prophetic Voices* (Minneapolis: Augsburg Fortress, 2000).

[2]Eugene Peterson, *Subversive Spirituality* (Grand Rapids: Eerdmans, 1997), 207.

[3]Barbara Brown Taylor, *An Altar in the World* (New York: HarperCollins, 2009).

[4]Esther de Waal, *Seeking God: The Way of St. Benedict* (Collegeville, MN: Liturgical Press, 1984), 30.

[5]Annie Dillard, *Pilgrim at Tinker Creek* (New York: HarperCollins, 1974), 274.

[6]Walter Brueggemann, *Prayers for a Privileged People* (Nashville: Abingdon, 2008), 51.

[7]From http://marshill.org/teaching-resources/spiritual-practices/#. However, this is no longer posted on the website.

CHAPTER 9: RABBI

[1]From *Max Weber: Essays in Sociology*, trans. and ed. H. H. Gerth and C. Wright Mills (New York: Oxford University Press, 1946), 155.

[2]Henri J. M. Nouwen, *The Way of the Heart: Desert Spirituality and Contemporary Ministry* (New York: Ballantine, 1981), 15-16.

[3]See his talk at www.cnn.com/2010/OPINION/10/10/treasure.sound.

[4]Mother Teresa, *A Simple Path* (New York: Random House, 1995), 7.

[5]Ibid., 26.

[6]Richard Foster, *Celebration of Discipline: The Path to Spiritual Growth* (New York: HarperCollins, 1978) 20.

CHAPTER 10: ACCENT

[1]Sharon Daloz Parks, *Big Questions, Worthy Dreams: Mentoring Emerging Adults in Their Search for Meaning, Purpose, and Faith* (San Francisco: Jossey-Bass, 2011), 116.

[2]Richard Foster, *Streams of Living Water* (San Francisco: HarperCollins, 2001).

[3]Daniel James Brown, *Boys in the Boat: Nine Americans and Their Epic Quest for Gold at the 1936 Berlin Olympics* (New York: Viking Penguin, 2013), 90.

CONCLUSION

[1] Brennan Manning, *Abba's Child: The Cry of the Heart for Intimate Belonging* (Colorado Springs: NavPress, 1994), 99.

[2] Cornel West, *Hope on a Tightrope* (Carlsbad, CA: Smiley, 2008), 41.

[3] Annie Dillard, *Pilgrim at Tinker Creek* (New York: HarperCollins, 1974), 10.

SCRIPTURE INDEX

formatio

TRADITION. EXPERIENCE.
TRANSFORMATION.

Formatio books from InterVarsity Press follow the rich tradition of the church in the journey of spiritual formation. These books are not merely about being informed, but about being transformed by Christ and conformed to his image. Formatio stands in InterVarsity Press's evangelical publishing tradition by integrating God's Word with spiritual practice and by prompting readers to move from inward change to outward witness. InterVarsity Press uses the chambered nautilus for Formatio, a symbol of spiritual formation because of its continual spiral journey outward as it moves from its center. We believe that each of us is made with a deep desire to be in God's presence. Formatio books help us to fulfill our deepest desires and to become our true selves in light of God's grace.